CRITICAL PUBLISHING

The Higher Education

Personal Tutor's and Advisor's Companion

TRANSLATING THEORY INTO PRACTICE TO IMPROVE STUDENT SUCCESS

Edited by Dave Lochtie, Andrew Stork and Ben W Walker

Foreword by Dr Emily McIntosh and Professor Liz Thomas

In association with UKAT UKAT

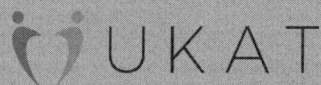

First published in 2022 by Critical Publishing Ltd

British Library Cataloguing in Publication Data
A CIP record for this book is available from the British Library

ISBN: 978-1-913453-45-9

This book is also available in the following e-book formats:

EPUB ISBN: 978-1-913453-47-3
Adobe e-book ISBN: 978-1-913453-48-0

Cover design by Out of House Limited
Text design by Greensplash Limited
Project Management by Newgen Publishing UK
Printed and bound in Great Britain by 4edge, Essex

Critical Publishing
3 Connaught Road
St Albans
AL3 5RX
www.criticalpublishing.com
Paper from responsible sources

The Higher Education

Personal Tutor's and Advisor's Companion

TRANSLATING THEORY INTO PRACTICE TO IMPROVE STUDENT SUCCESS

To order, or for details of our bulk discounts, please go to our website www.criticalpublishing.com or contact our distributor, Ingram Publisher Services (IPS UK), 10 Thornbury Road, Plymouth PL6 7PP, telephone 01752 202301 or email IPSUK.orders@ingramcontent.com.

Contents

Meet the editors

Dave Lochtie

I am the Operations Manager for the Personal Learning Advisory Service at the Open University, which provides targeted one-to-one support for student populations identified in the institution's Access and Participation plan. I am Chair of the UK Advising and Tutoring association (UKAT), which supports personal tutors and academic advisors across the UK, as well as Co-chair of the Association for Peer Learning and Support, which promotes best practice in student-led learning. I am a qualified teacher and co-author of *Effective Personal Tutoring in Higher Education*. I have worked in student services management roles at the University of Derby and University of New Orleans as well as serving as an elected Director, Trustee and Governor of the University of Roehampton and Bournemouth University Students' Union. I am passionate about student voice, engagement, support and success.

Andrew Stork

I am a University Teacher and Programme Director for the Postgraduate Certificate in Medical Education within the Academic Unit of Medical Education at the University of Sheffield. I am co-author of two highly regarded texts for Critical Publishing, a Senior Fellow of the Higher Education Academy and have presented at national and international conferences on personal tutoring. I have experience of a wide range of educational sectors and contexts, and have led and taught on postgraduate education programmes across a variety of sectors. Previously, I was cross-institutional quality lead for personal tutoring and student experience, and have held a broad range of curriculum leadership, quality, teaching enhancement and staff development positions. I believe in and advocate a holistic approach to students and their education which can transform lives.

Ben W Walker

I am a Senior Lecturer in Educational Development within the Oxford Centre for Academic Enhancement and Development at Oxford Brookes University where I support colleagues to gain fellowship of the Higher Education Academy, deliver staff development and undertake educational research projects. Previously holding positions at the University of Lincoln, Manchester Metropolitan University and the University of Derby, I have supported a wide range of trainee teachers and existing practitioners. I have been programme leader of the Postgraduate Certificate in Learning and Teaching in Higher Education and been an invited keynote speaker at national and international conferences. As co-author of books and journal articles on personal tutoring, I am at the forefront of professional development and research in this field and am committed to developing it further.

Editors' websites

To find out more about the editors' work, visit their websites.

Dave Lochtie: www.davelochtie.com

Andrew Stork: www.andrewstork.co.uk

Ben W Walker: www.benwwalker.co.uk

Acknowledgements and dedication

Acknowledgements

We would like to thank:

- the authors of these case studies for their commitment and contributions to this book as well as to tutoring and advising practice;

- our families, for getting us through when it was difficult, being patient in our absence and for their unwavering support;

- Julia Morris for her continuing advice and support;

- Emily McIntosh and Liz Thomas for providing the foreword and the published works referenced throughout;

- the UK Advising and Tutoring association (UKAT), which this volume was produced in association with.

Dedication

To Hannah, Willow, Violet, May, Mum, David and the Dream Team.
DL

To Lorna, Josh and Jake who inspire me, and to all those who seek to inspire others, whilst standing at their side.
AS

To Petra, Sisi and Carly.
BW

A note on the text and terminology

This book is a companion to *Effective Personal Tutoring in Higher Education* (2018). Practitioners across the sector have translated its key themes, theories and concepts, as well as additional areas of personal tutoring practice and management, into real-world practice through case study narratives about how they have improved student outcomes and practice.

In the 2018 book we used the term 'personal tutor' to encapsulate the wide range of tutoring roles that frequently exist within universities, such as 'academic advisor', 'student advisor', 'progress tutor' or 'student support officer'. The terms 'personal tutor' and 'advisor' have been used in the title of this text to better reflect the full diversity of those used in the case studies. The former is only used in approximately half of them and the latter in several, with a few other terms used including 'personal academic tutor', 'personal development tutor' and 'academic mentor'. On occasion, some case studies use 'tutor' as an abbreviation of 'personal tutor'. As is explored in the case studies, the definitions and boundaries of these titles differ from one institution to another but we feel their similarities are substantial enough to merit grouping and comparison, with an awareness of those differences.

As in the 2018 book, the term 'at risk' is used in several case studies to describe students who may face additional barriers to succeed in their studies. The term is used with an awareness of its complexity and potential limitations, as outlined in the 2018 book and considered in one of the case studies (Hannam and Dalrymple, Case study 12).

The term Postgraduate Certificate in Learning and Teaching in Higher Education is used in this text as an umbrella term referring to postgraduate-level qualifications related to learning and teaching. This is done with an awareness of the variety of titles used for similar programmes across the sector such as Postgraduate Certificate in Academic Practice, Postgraduate Certificate in Teaching in Higher Education and Academic Professional Apprenticeship.

Foreword

The UK approach to personal tutoring and academic advising has long been in need of a thorough overhaul. As highlighted in Lochtie et al's 2018 monograph *Effective Personal Tutoring in Higher Education*, models and systems of tutoring and advising have remained fairly stagnant since the 1960s, yet the sector itself has not. Almost four years since that publication, the challenges associated with tutoring and advising not only remain, they have been exacerbated. The original conception of tutoring and advising as a bastion of one-to-one and personalised support has become extremely difficult to manage and make coherent in an increasingly massified, diversified and online academy.

We have now reached a critical juncture. The Covid-19 pandemic and the widespread sector-wide adoption of blended approaches to learning and teaching since March 2020 have expedited and made urgent the need to acknowledge advising as core pedagogical practice, central to the student experience and success. We now need to: (a) understand and emphasise the fundamental purpose of personal tutoring and advising in UK universities, (b) work towards outlining the national evidence base and create a framework upon which models, principles and systems of high-quality tutoring and advising can be outlined and adopted, and (c) highlight and champion how advising can help the sector to develop and diversify the curriculum to meet the needs of our students and improve their educational experience and outcomes in a post-pandemic world. Sector-wide leadership is absolutely necessary to realise this – to effectively reconstitute the purpose of tutoring and advising to ensure it can best realise its potential, that is to improve inclusion and student success across the breadth of UK higher education providers. With relationships at the forefront of blended approaches, the negotiation of multiple modalities and hybrid forms of learning, advising and tutoring become even more fundamental to the curation of the future learning experience – for both individuals and cohorts.

As this volume of case studies attests, there is not a single aspect of the educational student experience that tutoring and advising does not touch – it is pervasively proximate in the experiences of thousands of UK students from a multitude of backgrounds, cultures and educational paradigms. At the beginning of this volume, the editors posit that "a new academic could be forgiven for thinking that personal tutoring and advising does not matter that much". This historic failure of the sector to understand and articulate the importance of tutoring and advising to learning and teaching cannot, in good faith, continue. The 25 case studies in this volume cover, in breadth and in depth, a large number of themes which dominate sector discourse around learning, teaching and the student experience. The theories, models, concepts and principles explored in the 2018 volume are here brought alive and applied in context, contributing to the evidence base for positioning tutoring and advising at the centre of the curriculum, indeed as student-centred pedagogy.

Several case studies explore macro considerations around this core topic, from establishing institutional and sector wide strategy and direction, to considering the language and terminology of advising, exploring the fundamental concepts of student transition, belonging and connectedness (at a time where, still in the midst of a global pandemic, these are more important than ever before) and approaches to evaluation. Others offer more detailed exploration of particular facets of tutoring and advising practice: considering solutions-focused coaching, the format of sessions, working with vulnerable groups, promoting employability, alignment with wider student support systems, student engagement and even co-creation. Several consider the importance of tutors and advisors themselves – approaches to academic and reflective practice, consideration of identities and purpose, and developing communities around advising.

The challenge of rewarding and recognising tutoring and advising remains, and it requires further exploration if we are to realise the potential of this work on students, and encourage investment in developing high-quality practice that makes an impact. More work is also required to consider the importance of tutoring and advising for diversifying and improving the inclusivity and accessibility of the curriculum. As regulation and policy making in UK higher education remain volatile, the time is now to establish tutoring and advising as a key approach to improving the student experience, and we need to get it right for our colleagues and our students. We welcome and celebrate this very important opportunity to look at tutoring and advising practice across the sector at this hugely critical time in the evolution of the HE sector.

Dr Emily McIntosh,
Director of Learning, Teaching and Student Experience at
Middlesex University

Professor Liz Thomas,
Independent higher education researcher and consultant
and Professor of Higher Education at Edge Hill University

Introduction

A new academic could be forgiven for thinking that personal tutoring and advising does not matter that much. The prevailing culture they enter may convey that this is one of the easy parts of the multiple demands of their occupation, a chance to escape the constraints of curriculum pressure and naturally chat to students about 'how everything is going'. Some staff see it as '*straight forward and unchallenging*' so training on it is not needed (Brown and Thomas, Case study 5); indeed, other than asking them how they are, what else is there to say? (Robinson, 2012). A senior leader at a university we recently visited openly stated that personal tutoring came tenth on an academic's priority list. It can be '*taken-for-granted*' (Stephen et al, 2008, p 449), is perceived as a skill inherent within lecturers (Owen, 2002, p 15) and it is assumed that personal tutors '*will know what to do*' (McFarlane, 2016, p 86). These descriptions seem misplaced, however. According to research, once undertaking the role, its tacit nature can initiate uncertainty and anxiety rather than any sense of liberation, as summed up by tutors in McFarlane's (2016) research: '*What am I supposed to be doing differently?*' and '*Actually, what do I do?*' (p 83). This appears to be something equally felt by students; one of our case studies characterises the act of personal tutoring as: '*Two people in a room that neither wants to be in for a purpose that is unclear to both*' (Powell and Prowse, Case study 17). Yet, its importance only seems to grow with the increasingly diverse needs presented by students in the context of the 'massification' of higher education seen in recent years.

Moreover, at an institutional and policy level, surely personal tutoring plays a major role in meeting the Teaching Excellence Framework metrics which higher education institutions are judged against: retention, progression, employability, a '*high-quality academic experience*' and '*value for money*' (OfS, 2018, p 14)? Its significance is underlined by key research which indicates the 'human side' of education comes first with proactive holistic support as the way to achieve the 'belonging' at the heart of student retention and success (Thomas, 2012; Thomas et al, 2017) and to combat persistent differences in student outcomes for 'at risk' groups (Mountford-Zimdars et al, 2015; OfS, 2019a, b; Universities UK/NUS, 2019).

So, personal tutoring's significance should not be in doubt. And yet, as many of our conversations and several studies show, it struggles for attention, remaining a poor relation to teaching and other academic activities. Effective practice is often ill-defined locally, which may explain its widespread status in institutions as 'under review', and its convenience for policy makers to use in combatting the many challenges faced by institutions.

In response to this, clarity and support are needed for practitioners, co-ordinators and policy makers alike. The current higher education context is characterised by varying and distinct student needs which demand that our professional skills be multi-faceted. While some colleagues increasingly have access to initial and continuing teaching-related development opportunities, these can be fewer for personal tutoring given the competing pressures on time and resources. Therefore, it deserves greater attention and a community of practitioners who are both supportive and supported.

Considering the following definition of the personal tutor – '*one who improves the intellectual and academic ability, and nurtures the emotional well-being of learners through individualised, holistic support*' (Stork and Walker, 2015, p 3) – we can hardly classify this activity as unimportant, straightforward or unchallenging. The aforementioned developments, combined with the impact of the Covid-19 pandemic, demonstrate that belonging and connectedness have arguably never been more vital and their key agents, personal tutors, never more crucial.

Where is personal tutoring and advising, and the literature surrounding it, at present? Since Thomas and Hixenbaugh brought together research from a range of universities in their 2006 publication, *Personal Tutoring in Higher Education*, further work appeared intermittently reflecting the sporadic attention personal tutoring received. Institutional and discipline-based studies, mainly on a small scale, have conveyed the importance and value of personal tutoring but arguably few demonstrate impact in terms of student outcomes. *Becoming an Outstanding Personal Tutor: Supporting Learners Through Personal Tutoring and Coaching* (2015) and the subsequent *Effective Personal Tutoring in Higher Education* (2018) aimed to fill the hitherto absence of practitioner texts underpinned by theory and research. In 2015, the UK Advising and Tutoring association (UKAT) was formed. The well-established *UK Professional Standards Framework* (UKPSF) (Advance HE, 2011) makes, arguably, only broad reference to student support methods and UKAT established a discrete set of professional standards and associated recognition awards in 2019 (UKAT, 2019) to specifically focus upon advising and tutoring. Most recently, *Academic Advising and Tutoring for Student Success in Higher Education: International Perspectives* aimed to strengthen the evidence base for practice and '*to acknowledge the centrality of high quality advising and tutoring to teaching, learning and student success*' (McIntosh et al, 2021, p 1). Hence, recently we have witnessed a heartening renaissance in research, development and support for personal tutoring.

Contemporary personal tutoring has been characterised by increasing diversity in the sector, re-evaluations of the relationship between institutions and students along with continual reviewing of tutorial arrangements. Diversifying models of delivering support have increasingly blurred the boundaries between academic and professional services as manifest in the multiple role titles given to the work. The onset of the Covid-19 pandemic, and the associated move to online and blended tutoring has foregrounded student well-being, engagement and belonging further. With opportunities for relational working and face-to-face learning less available (McIntosh, 2021), much discussion about, and support for, creating a sense of belonging and connectedness in a virtual world has taken place. It has arguably made supportive learning conversations more critical than ever.

Embodying these current trends, the case studies presented here aim to translate theory into practice and offer windows through which to gain insight and critically view what is happening in the sector. After publishing the first monograph on UK higher education personal tutoring in 12 years, we felt the need to further respond to the aforementioned challenges, dilemmas and tensions by illustrating its themes, theories and concepts, as well as additional areas of personal tutoring practice and leadership. Collating 'what works' in terms of impact on student and institutional outcomes, the intention is to enable transferability and promote the feeling of a national community of practice in an area which has not benefitted from extensive sharing of practice compared to teaching.

Our previous publications have discussed personal tutoring and teaching as intertwined yet different and, indeed, earlier studies *'clearly show HE teachers' views on tutoring's particular demands and requirements along with gaps in training and support'* (Walker, 2020, p 2). We recognise both personal tutoring's distinctive nature and, as one of our case studies situates it (McIntosh et al, Case study 14), its status as 'relational pedagogy' which puts positive relationships at the heart of teaching (Bovill, 2020). Indeed, we argue such a relational approach is not only the responsibility of teachers but that it is the responsibility of those across multiple 'advising' roles (including colleagues in professional services) to form an ethos of individualised, holistic student-centred support across the whole institution. This collection, as with the 2018 book before it, presents themes common to all advising roles and promotes the transferability of effective practice, being aimed at *'all activities where academic or professional staff work in partnership with students to provide one-to-one support, advice and guidance, of either an academic or pastoral nature'* (Lochtie et al, 2018, p 2).

The case studies come in a variety of forms, from personal stories of practice to action research and scholarly enquiry, with a broad range of perspectives provided by authors employed both in a range of academic and professional service roles, and universities. Their topics reflect current research, practice and leadership, highlighting their interdependence. Some are longitudinal and include evaluations of the impact of the actions taken, whereas others present more recent developments captured at an earlier stage and detail future planned evaluations.

Such variety results in some different terminology use and may at times present some divergent views. Indeed, the editors, authors and readers may not always fully agree with the approaches taken and views expressed. However, the case studies have more in common than what separates them and, more importantly, they share evidence-based ideas about positively influencing student success.

To aid your understanding and learning, critical reflection questions follow each case study and we have categorised them under the following four broad thematic areas, each of which contain sub-themes (see the following Themes section for a full list and how they connect with the companion book).

Several case studies explore **models of personal tutoring and advising**, with significant sub-themes including boundaries between roles, institutional review and implementation, and perspectives on role types (expert versus generalist; senior and specialised). The reader is asked to reflect on the potential merits of such models in their own context.

Discussions on a diverse range of **personal tutoring and advising practice** are presented, among them coaching, embedding within teaching and group approaches. While each case study offers its own unique perspective, collectively they represent a snapshot of leading practices across the field of personal tutoring and how they can be utilised to develop students.

Supporting students and student populations is considered in many of the case studies through examining topics including developing belonging, differentiation at individual, population and subject levels, as well as the provision of pastoral, transition and well-being support. The categorisation of students, such as the use of the complex 'at risk' label, is discussed by case studies within the volume.

Finally, the **development of personal tutoring and advising** is the focus of numerous case studies. They explore themes such as current design, definitions, values and research along with how professional development can enhance the field in the future.

What comes next? We hope that this collection is a noteworthy step in addressing the absence of studies which evidence the impact of personal tutoring and advising. However, there are significant areas for further work and, arguably, the ambition should be to build towards achieving a body of literature (and associated development) on a par with the wealth of such which exists for teaching. Important strides forward in meeting this challenge have already been made by a content analysis of global advising literature (Troxel et al, 2021). Future work on both the themes directly discussed within the case studies and the questions raised by them is necessary. Among these are effective conversational techniques, post-Covid-19 blended learning, the relationship between personal tutoring and teaching, personal tutoring as relational pedagogy (and links with other pedagogies), the involvement of students' perspectives and outcomes, and the relative status of tutoring in the overall role of an 'academic'. Only then will practice be more evidence-based and the status of tutoring and advising raised to its rightful place.

The Editors

References

Advance HE (2011) *UK Professional Standards Framework for Teaching and Supporting Learning in Higher Education*. [online] Available at: www.heacademy.ac.uk/system/files/downloads/ukpsf_2011_english.pdf (accessed 1 October 2021).

Bovill, C (2020) *Co-creating Learning and Teaching: Towards Relational Pedagogy in Higher Education*. St Albans: Critical Publishing.

Lochtie D, McIntosh E, Stork A and Walker B W (2018) *Effective Personal Tutoring in Higher Education*. St Albans: Critical Publishing.

McFarlane, K J (2016) Tutoring the Tutors: Supporting Effective Personal Tutoring. *Active Learning in Higher Education*, 17(1): 77–88.

McIntosh E (2021) It's Not What You Do It's The Way That You Learn It – That's What Gets Results. *Build Back Higher: Dialogue and Community Will Return to Post-Covid Learning.* [online] Available at: https://wonkhe.com/blogs/build-back-higher-learning-2 (accessed 1 October 2021).

McIntosh, E, Thomas, L, Troxel, W G, van den Wijngaard, O and Grey, D (2021) Editorial: Academic Advising and Tutoring for Student Success in Higher Education: International Approaches. *Frontiers in Education*, 6: 631265.

Mountford-Zimdars, A, Sabri, D, Moore, J, Sanders, J, Jones, S and Higham, L (2015) *Causes of Differences in Student Outcomes.* Bristol: HEFCE.

Office for Students (OfS) (2018) *Securing Student Success: Regulatory Framework for Higher Education in England.* [online] Available at: www.officeforstudents.org.uk/media/1406/ofs2018_01.pdf (accessed 10 December 2021).

Office for Students (OfS) (2019a) Access and Participation Dashboard. [online] Available at: www.officeforstudents.org.uk/data-and-analysis/access-andparticipation-data-dashboard (accessed 1 October 2021).

Office for Students (OfS) (2019b) New Data Reveals University Performance on Access and Student Success. [online] Available at: www.officeforstudents.org.uk/news-blogand-events/press-and-media/new-data-reveals-university-performance-onaccess-and-student-success (accessed 1 October 2021).

Owen, M (2002) 'Sometimes You Feel You're in Niche Time': The Personal Tutor System, A Case Study. *Active Learning in Higher Education*, 3(1): 7–23.

Robinson, P (2012) *Leeds for Life: Preparing Our Students for Their Future.* [online] Available at: https://nacada.ksu.edu/Resources/Academic-Advising-Today/View-Articles/Leeds-for-Life-Preparing-Our-Students-for-Their-Future.aspx (accessed 1 October 2021)

Stephen, D E, O'Connell, P and Hall, M (2008) 'Going the Extra Mile', 'Fire-fighting', or *Laissez-faire*? Re-evaluating Personal Tutoring Relationships within Mass Higher Education. *Teaching in Higher Education*, 13(4): 449–60.

Stork, A and Walker, B (2015) *Becoming an Outstanding Personal Tutor: Supporting Learners Through Personal Tutoring and Coaching.* St Albans: Critical Publishing.

Thomas, L (2012) *Building Student Engagement and Belonging in Higher Education at a Time of Change. Final Report from the What Works? Student Retention and Success Programme.* [online] Available at: www.heacademy.ac.uk/sites/default/files/resources/What_works_final_report.pdf (accessed 10 December 2021).

Thomas, L and Hixenbaugh, P (2006) *Personal Tutoring in Higher Education.* Stoke-on-Trent: Trentham Books.

Thomas, L, Hill, M, O'Mahony, J and Yorke, M (2017) *Supporting Student Success: Strategies for Institutional Change. What Works? Student Retention and Success Programme. Final Report.* [online] Available at: www.advance-he.ac.uk/knowledge-hub/supporting-student-success-strategies-institutional-change (accessed 10 October 2021).

Troxel, W G, Rubin, L, Grey, D and McIntosh, E (2021) *Content Analysis of 15 Years of Advising-related Research in Higher Education*. Research Report, NACADA Center for Research, Kansas State University.

UKAT (UK Advising and Tutoring) (2019) The UKAT Professional Framework for Advising and Tutoring. [online] Available at: www.ukat.uk/professional-development/professional-framework-for-advising-and-tutoring (accessed 1 October 2021).

Universities UK/NUS (2019) *Black, Asian and Minority Ethnic Student Attainment at UK Universities: #ClosingTheGap*. Report. London: UUK. [online] Available at: www.universitiesuk.ac.uk/sites/default/files/field/downloads/2021-07/bame-student-attainment.pdf (accessed 18 December 2021).

Walker, B W (2020) Professional Standards and Recognition for UK Personal Tutoring and Advising. *Frontiers in Education*. [online] Available at: https://doi.org/10.3389/feduc.2020.531451 (accessed 14 January 2022).

Themes

The four tables below illustrate the main and sub-themes covered in the collection by case study and by their locations in the companion book *Effective Personal Tutoring in Higher Education* (2018).

While the case studies can be read in a linear order, the presentation of these themes is intended to aid you in identifying the key areas relevant to you in your specific role. The case studies are presented in alphabetical order by lead author rather than grouped by theme because, rather than focusing on one theme only, each contains a varying level of focus spread over a range of themes.

Table T.1 *Models of personal tutoring and advising*

Models of personal tutoring and advising	Case study	Page number locations in the companion book
Boundaries between roles	2, 7, 10, 11, 14, 15, 17, 23, 25	53–73
Centralised model	19, 21	21–2
Faculty/school/department-level perspective	18, 21	23
Framework of personal tutoring and advising	7, 17	23–5
Institutional review and implementation	4, 7, 8, 10, 11, 13, 15, 17, 21	23–5
Role types – expert versus generalist; senior and specialised personal tutor and advisor	1, 5, 7, 11, 15, 19, 20, 21, 25	22–3
Supplementary support for personal tutoring and advising	2, 3, 15, 16, 23	22
Whole-institution approach	5, 14, 15	24

Table T.2 *Personal tutoring and advising practice*

Personal tutoring and advising practice	Case study	Page number locations in the companion book
Careers and employability	1, 2, 6, 7	122–7
Coaching	4, 5, 6, 9, 17, 23	15–21, 136–52
Embedded into teaching	1, 5, 14, 18, 19, 24	22
Group personal tutoring and advising	4, 5, 8, 14, 16, 20, 24	114–17
Personal tutoring and advising curriculum	7, 14, 24	122–8
Student involvement and co-creation	2, 4, 8, 9, 10, 13, 16, 17, 24,	61, 107, 116, 167–8
Student peer support	1, 9, 23, 24	61, 107, 116
Student reflective practice	1, 11, 13	43, 116

Table T.3 *Supporting students and student populations*

Supporting students and student populations	Case study	Page number locations in the companion book
Data analytics	3, 12, 14	92–5
Developing a sense of belonging among students	2, 3, 4, 10, 12, 14, 16, 22, 23, 24	13
Differentiating by individual student needs	3, 4, 6, 12	108–14
Differentiating by student population	1, 3, 12, 14, 18, 21	75–85
Differentiating by subject area	8, 10, 13, 17, 20, 25	–
Pastoral support	7, 13, 19, 20	21–2, 56
Programme perspective	1, 13, 20	24, 45–6
Student engagement	1, 4, 14, 15, 18, 23, 24	44, 56–60, 66–7
Transition	3, 8, 14, 17, 18, 19, 20	105–8
Well-being	2, 12, 14, 23	13, 23, 55, 179–80

Table T.4 *Development of personal tutoring and advising*

Development of personal tutoring and advising	Case study	Page number locations in the companion book
Experiential design	4	158–9
Personal tutor and advisor forums	7, 10, 11, 25	–
Postgraduate Certificate in Learning and Teaching in Higher Education	10, 22	4
Problem-based learning	22	–
Reflective practice	6, 8, 9, 22, 25	153–67, 170–1
Research and evaluation	8, 16, 17, 19, 20	4, 12, 175–98
Role definition	5, 14, 25	12–14
Training/professional development	2, 5, 7, 8, 9, 12	167–71
Values in personal tutoring and advising	1, 9, 22, 25	32–9

Case study 1
Supporting student employability through integrated research exposure and a curriculum-embedded skills module

Jean Assender and Wendy Leadbeater

Themes	Page number locations in the companion book
Careers and employability	122–7
Embedded into teaching	22
Programme perspective	24, 45–6
Role types – expert versus generalist; senior and specialised personal tutor and advisor	22–3
Student engagement	44, 56–60, 66–7
Student peer support	61, 107, 116
Student reflective practice	3, 116
Supporting student populations	75–85
Values in personal tutoring and advising	32–9

Introduction

Graduate employability is not only a key matrix by which universities and programmes are measured (Jackson, 1999; Knight and Yorke, 2001), but happy, successful graduates are the ultimate goal of academic advising and tutoring, and graduate employability is one facet of that. A good academic tutor will provide information about higher education processes, procedures and expectations, pastoral support, and referral to other professional services (Thomas, 2006; Lochtie et al, 2018). This will help students to succeed academically but does it improve employability post-graduation? Embedding early and frequent authentic research in an undergraduate science programme positively correlates with improved retention and successful graduation, particularly for STEM (science, technology, engineering and maths) subjects (Jones et al, 2010). It has also been shown to benefit students' ability to think independently, formulate ideas and increases their intrinsic motivation to learn (Lopatto, 2010). We sought to investigate whether embedding these real-life experiences and employability skills training, along with opportunities for reflection with their personal academic tutor (PAT), would provide students with 'critical moments' leading to change in their career and educational trajectory (Yair, 2009).

The Personal Academic Development module at the University of Birmingham

The BSc Biomedical Sciences programme at the University of Birmingham admits students with three A levels (grade BBB) plus widening participation students through 'Access to Birmingham' (a programme which supports applicants who have little or no experience of higher education). In 2014, the personal tutoring system was pastoral (Lochtie et al, 2018) and career support peripheral to the academic content. Fifty-nine per cent of incoming students (questionnaire response rate = 67.5 per cent) listed 'study medicine' as one of their career aspirations. Only 14 per cent reported aspiring to pursue a higher degree or research-focused career, while 20 per cent of students had no specific career plans. Graduate-level employment rates were lower than average.

Employability is a multidimensional concept made up of students' personal qualities (for example, self-efficacy/initiative), core skills (for example, information retrieval, critical evaluation) and process skills (for example, prioritising, computer literacy) (Lees, 2002). To be effective, learners need to learn and apply these skills in a variety of different situations integrated throughout their course (Yorke, 2001). We developed a Personal Academic Development (PAD) module which ran throughout all three years of their programme. It provided a student-centred approach integrating academic and employability skills teaching (Lochtie et al, 2018) while creating a framework for students to reflect on their development (Schön, 1983). Through discussion with their PATs, students were encouraged to reflect on their experience (Kolb, 1984) within a supportive environment (Meyers and Nulty, 2009).

Approach and implementation of an integrated curriculum supported by personal tutoring

To improve students' awareness and motivation to pursue alternative careers, we embedded early exposure to research and academic skills in a first-year 'Introduction to Research and Experimental Skills' (IRES) module. In parallel, the PAD module (supported through the personal tutoring system) provided a portfolio of authentic and timely activities that aligned with key events in the curriculum (laboratory competence, reflection on assessment feedback, goal setting, careers events and reflection on skills development). We trained and supported our colleagues, including PATs, academic teachers and early career researchers, as they were key to supporting and promoting students' personal and professional development. The early career researchers were able to share their current research expertise and career experiences, offering the benefit of near-peer teaching, which has been shown to be an effective model of teaching and learning that benefits both the learner and the teacher (Bulte et al, 2007; Cate and Durning, 2007). We used this near-peer approach in the IRES tutorials as the teachers had recently undertaken a similar degree programme and were able to support students while offering an approachable and empathetic attitude (Cate and Durning, 2007; Benè and Bergus, 2014). The integrated approach of IRES and PAD modules, illustrated in Figure 1.1, enabled students to meet, work with and learn from their peers, near-peer researchers, careers staff, PATs, as well as academic teaching staff, and had the following core objectives.

1.   Early and frequent exposure to authentic research through lab visits and inspirational talks by active researchers; school research strengths were introduced at an early stage and showcased at the research conference, inspiring young academics.

2.   Embedded academic and professional skills teaching, such as academic literacy, referencing, presentation skills, teamwork, experimental design, data analysis and statistics.

3.   Challenging, authentic assessments promoting deep learning. We provided 'sorting out difficulties' workshops for bespoke feedback, motivation and support with structuring their assessments.

4.   A framework to encourage students to articulate and reflect on their developing skills and career trajectory with careers staff and PATs through their portfolio (PAD module).

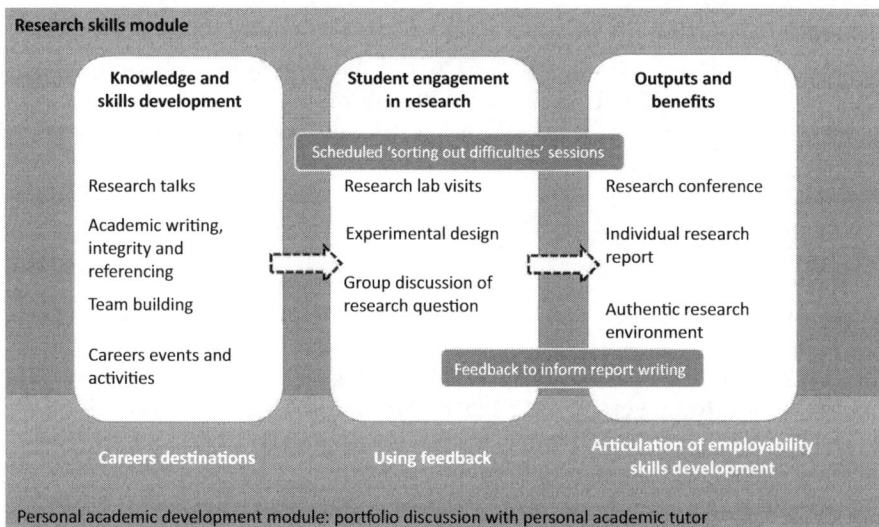

Figure 1.1 *Integration of the IRES and PAD modules*

The student-centred approach to the challenging research skills module assessment (Figure 1.2) enabled student groups to develop a research strategy aligned to their lab visit and research question, supported by an academic tutor and their peers. The group then applied their newly acquired knowledge and skills to present at the research conference, gaining feedback, which they could feed-forward to their individual assessed report.

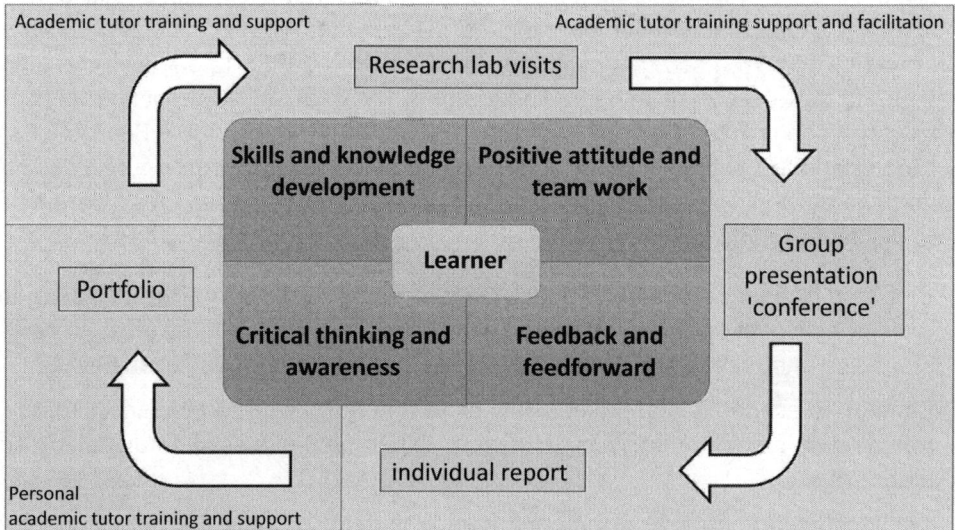

Figure 1.2 *The student-centred approach to the research skills module assessment*

The learner is central to the authentic research activities. Surrounded by a supportive environment, the student, through their academic tutors and PATs, engages in academic and team skills development. Providing training and continuing support to the early career researchers was important to ensure clear messaging and appropriate-level research questions were provided to students. Key to PAT engagement was training in tutoring core values (McFarlane, 2016; Lochtie et al, 2018), making the benefits of personal and academic development explicit (Hayes et al, 2016) and explaining how the PAD module integrated into the curriculum.

Evaluation and impact

Graduate-level employment rates improved

Introduction of these modules correlated with improved graduate-level (GL) employment rates (Table 1.1). Both 'first to university' and Black, Asian and Minority Ethnic (BAME) students particularly benefitted from the early and frequent research exposure and tailored support. While this does not unequivocally prove that supporting students to develop professional academic skills increases employability, the wider university's GL employability rates did not increase, suggesting that this was not due to some underlying trend.

Table 1.1 Graduate-level employment rates six months after graduation

Students	Pre-curriculum GL employment rate (%)	Post-curriculum GL employment rate (%)	Change (%)
Biomedical Sciences	73.7	83.3	+9.6
First to university	64.3	78.3	+ 14
BAME	71.4	87.5	+ 16.1
Whole university	86.7	85.8	-0.9

The figures in Table 1.1 are based on the Destination of Leavers from Higher Education survey for the student cohort pre-curriculum (graduating 2014) compared to the first cohort of students graduating under the new curriculum (graduating 2017). More recent data is non-comparable due to the change within the Graduate Outcomes Survey in 2018.

Identifying critical moments that influence career plans

Since introducing IRES and PAD modules, final-year student questionnaires showed that 40 per cent of students changed their career plans during their degree (Figure 1.3). Students responding 'yes' to the question on career aspirations clarified the nature of this change, the largest being from medicine to research.

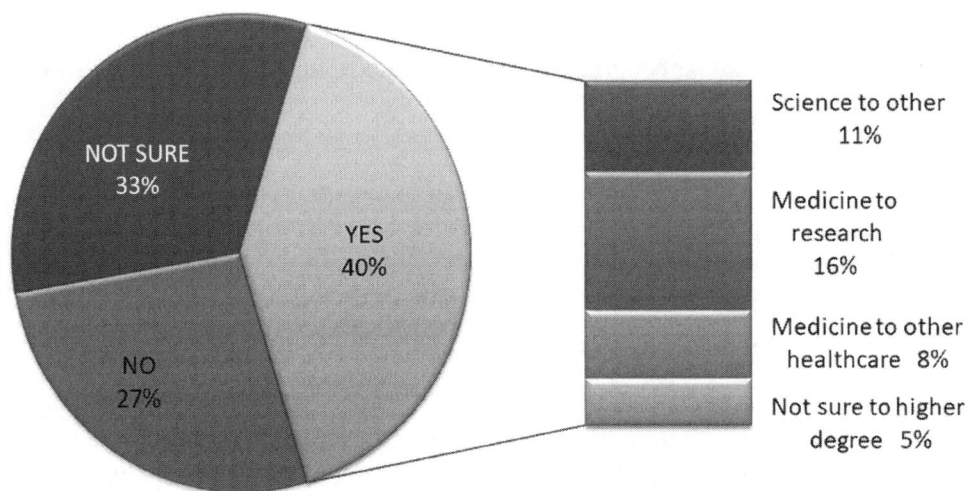

Figure 1.3 Students' responses to the question: 'Since starting the degree have your career aspirations changed?' (Students graduated in 2017; response rate = 38%)

In order to determine the impact of our interventions, we asked final-year students (cumulative data over three years 2017–19) what they felt were the critical moments (Yair, 2009) in their degree. They were inspired first and foremost by their final-year research project (84 per cent), summer internships (61 per cent), careers talks (60 per cent) and lab visits in year 1 (43 per cent). Their PATs (43 per cent) were also reported to have had a large impact on their decision making and positively influenced their post-graduation plans. Students who changed their career aspirations from medicine to research commented:

> *Triggered by curiosity, I undertook a summer research project... now have a PhD offer.*

> *... I am just into science more than into being a doctor, being a researcher is another way of helping people.*

One of the key innovations was the research lab visits in year 1, followed by the authentic assessment (research conference). Students commented:

> *Poster was surprisingly fun and intellectually challenging.*

> *Allowed me to gain insight into the life of a researcher.*

Early career researchers acting as academic tutors on the IRES module fed back:

> *This is just what I wish I had had when I was an undergraduate.*

> *I am quite disappointed not to be able to continue [tutoring next year], I had a great time and learnt a lot last year.*

Similar to previous findings, we found that embedding careers support into the mainstream provision (Thomas, 2012, p 20) facilitated better student engagement. Since the introduction of the PAD module, engagement increased year on year. In 2015–16, only 3.25 per cent of our students made appointments with careers colleagues, in 2016–17 = 34.6 per cent, 2017–18 = 44.3 per cent and 2018–19 = 44.9 per cent.

Conclusion

The integrated approach of a discipline-specific skills module using real-life research linked to authentic assessment, alongside the PAD module, provided students with feedback on their academic skills and empowered them to approach careers colleagues and PATs to discuss career aspirations. Students gained real-life experience, increasing their motivation to learn (Lopatto, 2010), while the portfolio aided articulation of their employability skills development (Mahmood et al, 2014). While the benefit of embedding academic skills into the curriculum for improved student performance has been widely acknowledged (Wingate, 2011; Minogue et al, 2018), our integrated approach had the additional benefit of improving GL employability. We know that students from minority backgrounds generally enter university less well equipped to successfully navigate educational pathways (Fries-Britt et al, 2010) and our approach seemed to particularly benefit 'first to university' and BAME students.

Developing links and collaboration was paramount for the success of our approach. Module leads developed collaborations with the following groups of staff.

1. Discipline-specific academic tutors and early career researchers, to ensure research questions were sufficiently focused and pitched to the correct level.

2. PATs, to be aware of the curriculum, assessments and PAD module, to support students in their personal academic development.

3. Careers colleagues, sharing curriculum information to allow relevant timely events and support to be embedded within the PAD module.

Key messages

- Work closely with and embed careers support into mainstream careers discussions.

- Provide early opportunities for students to engage with and meet researchers to provide motivating and insightful real-life experiences.

- Embed the personal tutoring system into the curriculum to align with skills development.

- Train and support tutors to share the values and rationale in order to support student engagement.

Critical reflections

1. How effective is your personal tutoring provision in supporting graduate employability and how might this be improved?

2. What training and development in supporting students with career planning do you think you need as a personal tutor? What would be the most effective way for this to happen?

3. How effectively are your personal tutoring activities linked with the curriculum? Where can this be enhanced further and how?

References

Benè, K L and Bergus, G (2014) When Learners Become Teachers: A Review of Peer Teaching in Medical Student Education. *Family Medicine*, 46(10): 783–7.

Bulte, C, Betts, A, Garner, K and Durning, S (2007) Student Teaching: Views of Student Near-peer Teachers and Learners. *Medical Teacher*, 29(6): 583–90.

Cate, O T and Durning, S (2007) Peer Teaching in Medical Education: Twelve Reasons to Move from Theory to Practice. *Medical Teacher*, 29(6): 591–9.

Fries-Britt, S L, Younger, T K and Hall, W D (2010) Lessons from High-achieving Students of Color in Physics. *The New Directions for Institutional Research*, 148: 75–83.

Hayes, C, Fulton, J, Devlin, S, Westwood, D, Garfield, I, Beardmore, P, Archer, D, Collins, M and Lewis, B (2016) Perception of Academic Learning Environments and Perceived Impact on Articulation of Employability Skills: A Mixed Methods Study. *Journal of Learning and Development in Higher Education*, 10: 1–19.

Jackson, N (1999) Modelling Change in a National HE System Using the Concept of Unification. *Journal of Education Policy*, 14(4): 411–34.

Jones, M T, Barlow, A E L and Villarejo, M (2010) Importance of Undergraduate Research for Minority Persistence and Achievement in Biology. *The Journal of Higher Education*, 81: 82–115.

Knight, P and Yorke, M (2001) Employability Through the Curriculum. *Tertiary Education and Management*, 8(4): 261–76.

Kolb, D (1984) *Experiential Learning: Experience as the Source of Learning and Development.* Englewood Cliffs, NJ: Prentice Hall.

Lees, D (2002) *Graduate Employability-Literature Review.* Publication of the LTSN Generic Centre. [online] Available at: www.qualityresearchinternational.com/esecttools/esectpubs/leeslitreview.pdf (accessed 10 December 2021).

Lochtie, D, McIntosh, E, Stork, A and Walker, B W (2018) *Effective Personal Tutoring in Higher Education.* St Albans: Critical Publishing.

Lopatto, D (2010) Undergraduate Research as a High Impact Student Experience. *Peer Review – Association of American Colleges and Universities*, 12(2): 27–30.

Mahmood, L, Slabu, L, Randsley de Moura, G and Hopthrow, T (2014) Employability in the First Degree: The Role of Work Placements on Students' Perceptions of Graduate Employability. *Psychology Teaching Review*, 20(2): 126–36.

McFarlane, K J (2016) Tutoring the Tutors: Supporting Effective Personal Tutoring. *Active Learning in Higher Education*, 17(7): 77–88.

Meyers, N M and Nulty, D D (2009) How to Use (Five) Curriculum Design Principles to Align Authentic Learning Environments, Assessment, Students' Approaches to Thinking and Learning Outcomes. *Assessment And Evaluation in Higher Education*, 34(5): 565–77.

Minogue, L, Murphy, C and Salmons, K (2018) Embedding Learning Development; A Model for Collaborative Practice. *Journal of Learning Development in Higher Education*, 13: April. [online] Available at: https://journal.aldinhe.ac.uk/index.php/jldhe/article/view/443/pdf (accessed 10 December 2021).

Schön, D (1983) *The Reflective Practitioner: How Professionals Think in Action.* New York: Basic Books.

Thomas, L (2006) Widening Participation and the Increased Need for Personal Tutoring. In Thomas, L and Hixenbaugh, P (eds) *Personal Tutoring in Higher Education* (pp 21–31). Stoke-on-Trent: Trentham Books.

Thomas, L (2012) *Building Student Engagement and Belonging in Higher Education at a Time of Change. Final Report from the What Works? Student Retention and Success Programme.* [online] Available at: www.heacademy.ac.uk/sites/default/files/resources/What_works_final_report.pdf (accessed 10 December 2021).

Wingate, U, Andon, N and Cogo, A (2011) Embedding Academic Writing Instruction into Subject Teaching: A Case Study. *Active Learning in Higher Education*, 12(1): 69–81.

Yair, G (2009) Cinderellas and Ugly Ducklings: Positive Turning Points in Students' Educational Careers—Exploratory Evidence and a Future Agenda. *British Educational Research Journal*, 35: 351–70.

Yorke, M (2001) *Employability in the First Cycle Higher Education. A Working Paper for the Skills* Plus *Project*. Liverpool: John Moores University.

Dr Jean Assender

Jean Assender is Lecturer in Biomedical Sciences at the University of Birmingham and Senior Tutor for the School of Biomedical Sciences, responsible for personal academic tutoring and industrial placements. She has held a variety of teaching, programme leadership, welfare and quality improvement roles. She is a Senior Fellow of the Higher Education Academy and a Recognised Senior Advisor within UKAT.

Dr Wendy Leadbeater

Wendy Leadbeater is Senior Lecturer in Personal and Professional Development and Interprofessional Education at Aston University for Aston Medical School and Aston Pharmacy School. She is a Senior Fellow of the Higher Education Academy. She leads on student support for Aston Medical School, where she is responsible for personal tutoring. Wendy has held a variety of teaching, tutoring, quality and programme leadership roles. She was previously Senior Lecturer in Medical Sciences at University of Birmingham and Senior Tutor for Biomedical Sciences.

Case study 2

The power of future planning: empowering personal tutors to have effective careers and employability conversations

Rosanna Ayton and Morag Walling

Themes	Page number locations in the companion book
Boundaries between roles	53–73
Careers and employability	122–7
Developing a sense of belonging among students	13
Student involvement and co-creation	61, 107, 116, 167–8
Supplementary support for personal tutoring and advising	22
Training/Professional development	167–71
Well-being	13, 23, 55, 179–80

Introduction

From 2019 the Personal Tutoring Manager and Embedding Employability Specialist from the Careers and Employability team at King's College London have collaborated to support personal tutors to have conversations with their tutees about future planning, career paths and next steps. Here we will share how this collaboration came about and has developed over time to encourage other personal tutoring teams to think about how they can work with internal specialist services to enhance both the students' and personal tutors' experience.

From a careers perspective it is known that students who explore and develop next-step plans during their time in higher education have better outcomes after graduation than those who do not (Department for Education, 2017) and it is acknowledged that there is *'inequity at this stage of individual progression'* (Universities UK, 2019, p 2). To try to redress this imbalance King's is exploring how to ensure that career and employability benefits are experienced more equitably across the whole student population.

It is broadly recognised that personal tutors are key contacts for having meaningful conversations, and that they can help students navigate the hidden rules of higher education and form networks (Mountford-Zimdars et al, 2015). These elements contribute to a sense of belonging which supports positive student well-being and attainment (Thomas, 2012). It therefore seems logical to utilise personal tutor meetings to engage students in future planning. This case study illustrates not only what we have done but how and why it might be of interest to other institutions.

Empowering personal tutors to have effective careers and employability conversations at King's

Why did we decide to collaborate?

At King's we use the pastoral model of personal tutoring (Earwaker, 1992), where meetings cover academic progress, checking in on student well-being and encouragement to engage in extracurricular and employability activities. When we asked the King's 100 – a diverse panel of students, reflective of the King's community, who co-create student experience initiatives – what they would like to see included in an ideal personal tutor meeting, one of the most common answers was around 'future plans' with the fifth most common answer being 'career suggestions'.

With this in mind, we have focused on how to support more meaningful personal tutoring conversations that allow discussion around future plans and enable staff to empower students to make their own decisions about their next steps so that students are encouraged to start their thinking in whatever space they feel comfortable. However, personal tutors are not expected to become careers experts. At King's we had already been moving towards ensuring that the employability value of the academic curriculum was more explicit for both students and academics, so this also presents an opportunity for personal tutors to have conversations more confidently about the knowledge, attributes and skills that students are developing through their academic experience.

How has the collaboration worked?

Inviting a member of the Careers and Employability team to be present at personal tutor training sessions supported our mutual understanding of the issues from different perspectives. There was significant interest when personal tutors were encouraged to consider what the predominant careers or employability issues and barriers might be for their cohort. This enabled colleagues to think differently about what their role in these conversations could be. When training moved online due to Covid-19 we utilised Padlet to encourage discussion and sharing of ideas. Using scenarios (for example, 'I need help with my CV', 'I don't want the pressure of deciding a career now') has proved effective for both in-person and online training as staff receive immediate feedback.

We also include careers and employability content routinely in the monthly newsletter to personal tutors, focusing on specific points of the student journey. This includes linking to a student-facing blog which interprets some of the less obvious benefits of engagement with careers and employability activities and resources, and is designed to appeal specifically to underrepresented groups, such as students from Black, Asian and Minority Ethnic backgrounds or those who are the first in their family to come to university.

Evidence for the usefulness of this approach

This approach has been developed through gaining a deeper understanding of why this type of conversation is useful for students as opposed to simply signposting to the Careers and Employability Service.

Firstly, taking steps towards your future turns out to be harder than we might think for young people (Blakemore, 2019). Blakemore (2019) identifies that the part of the brain that controls planning and decision making is less well developed than was previously understood, and therefore students may need their learning for this area to be appropriately supported within an educational context. Guiding personal tutors to ask their tutees clarifying questions helps them to better identify the type of support which may actually benefit a student. This is reflected in research conducted at King's in 2018 looking at the journey of our first-year undergraduate students, which identified that they generally did not engage in active forward planning and that ideas of careers seem distant and abstract.

Secondly, young people will use significant people around them to test out ideas for possible futures before getting to a point where they are ready to take action (Nurami, 1990). This is supported by what we are hearing from students – that they want more meaningful conversations, and that some are looking to start these conversations with their personal tutors in the first instance.

Finally, engaging in these conversations actively supports student well-being. Eudemonic well-being, which includes having a purpose in life and feelings around personal growth, is critical to achieving good overall well-being (Robertson, 2021). Empowering personal tutors to initiate and feel more comfortable having future-focused conversations with students subsequently supports students to develop strategies to achieve personal growth.

Outcomes to date

Feedback for the online personal tutor training showed that 70 per cent of staff (circa 41 participants) stated that they felt more confident supporting their tutees' engagement with employability skills after completing this training (the remainder felt the same as before). Less than 5 per cent of attendees said they found the careers and employability content useful in the in-person session. When considering this comparison, it should be noted that the in-person feedback came from a free text comment option on what attendees found useful in the training, whereas the online feedback specifically asked about staff confidence in particular areas. This suggests that asking specifically about confidence is a good method of evaluation, which also allows for direct comparisons as the training is further developed. It should also be considered that doing the training online may give more time for the learning to 'sink in' than attending an in-person session and giving feedback straightaway.

Conclusion

Our work to date has focused on increasing confidence in staff interactions with students as a first step in the process of addressing the wider issues highlighted at the beginning of this case study. From the personal tutoring perspective, collaborating with the Careers and Employability Service was effective in helping personal tutors feel more comfortable with the boundaries of their role because the message came from the experts in the area and was specifically tailored to the personal tutor context. Following this experience, we would recommend that other institutions consider collaborations with their internal specialist services, having found a similarly positive impact for personal tutors by strengthening the connection between them and our Counselling and Mental Health Service through interactive training sessions. For King's Careers and Employability Service in particular, this collaboration is supporting their institutional remit by reaching new student audiences who may be engaging initially with support at a more local level, and by better enabling all students to become more independent in their abilities to plan for their future.

This work has also helped personal tutors to see the wider value of future-focused conversations when supporting students in other areas of concern for a personal tutor such as academic progress and well-being. Conversations about future planning can complement those designed around academic progress by helping students think more holistically about what and why they are studying. This can help to build the staff–student relationship by discussing matters that both parties have a shared interest in. We also know that personal tutors can find supporting student welfare and well-being a daunting prospect that they may not feel fully equipped for (Byrom and Hughes, 2018). Highlighting topics of conversation that personal tutors may feel more comfortable with, for example around skills students can develop during their time in higher education that also support their future employability, and which can positively impact on their well-being, may help staff feel more confident in the role they can play in this area.

The collaboration has also helped to reduce the resistance that is sometimes felt towards initiatives that focus solely on student employability, as it can feel as though it detracts from the primary focus on academic endeavour. By bringing in careers and employability experts to help frame the conversations, we have helped personal tutors understand how these two elements support each other rather than seeing them as in tension.

Overall, our collaboration has demonstrated that, rather than duplicating the work a service is doing through personal tutoring, we can co-create something new that is mutually beneficial and plays to the strengths of our different areas and expertise, ultimately benefitting students more than if we were working in isolation. We would encourage our colleagues across the sector to think about the key areas of interest or concern for students and look at how collaboration between a specialist service and personal tutors may help to break down barriers to students accessing support, reach a wider range of students and develop strong professional relationships between services and academic staff that support the work done in each area.

Critical reflections

1. To what extent do you engage your students in meaningful future-focused conversations? Write down three open questions which would help your students to consider and clarify their future ambitions.

2. The case study identifies the importance of linking future-focused conversations with students' academic progress to help them think more holistically about their studies. For your practice and context, identify the specific key points in the students' journey when you may do this and how.

3. Across the student experience, identify specific areas where specialists (both internal and external) could support the development of personal tutoring provision. Which specialist will you contact first to collaborate with and why?

References

Blakemore, S (2019) *Inventing Ourselves: The Secret Life of the Teenage Brain*. London: Penguin Random House UK.

Department for Education (2017) *Planning for Success: Graduates' Career Planning and its Effect on Graduate Outcomes*. Bristol: HEFCE.

Earwaker, J (1992) *Helping and Supporting Students: Rethinking the Issues*. Buckingham: Society for Research into Higher Education and Open University Press.

Hughes, G, Panjwani, M, Tulcidas, P and Byrom, N (2018) *Student Mental Health: The Role and Experiences of Academics*. [online] Available at: www.studentminds.org.uk/uploads/3/7/8/4/3784584/180129_student_mental_health__the_role_and_experience_of_academics__student_minds_pdf.pdf (accessed 10 December 2021).

Mountford-Zimdars, A, Sabri, D, Moore, J, Sanders, J, Jones, S and Higham, L (2015) *Causes of Differences in Student Outcomes*. Bristol: HEFCE.

Nurami, J (1990) *How Do Adolescents See Their Future? A Review of the Development of Future Orientation and Planning*. [online] Available at: www.academia.edu/28495973/REVIEW_How_Do_Adolescents_See_Their_Future_A_Review_of_the_Development_of_Future_Orientation_and_Planning (accessed 10 December 2021).

Robertson, I (2021) What is Psychological Wellbeing? [online] Available at: www.robertsoncooper.com/blog/what-is-psychological-wellbeing (accessed 10 December 2021).

Thomas, L (2012) *Building Student Engagement and Belonging in Higher Education at a Time of Change. Final Report from the What Works? Student Retention and Success Programme.* [online] Available at: www.heacademy.ac.uk/sites/default/files/resources/What_works_final_report.pdf (accessed 10 December 2021).

Universities UK (2019) *Widening Opportunity in Higher Education – the Third Phase: Beyond Graduation.* [online] Available at: www.universitiesuk.ac.uk/what-we-do/policy-and-research/publications/widening-opportunity-higher-education (accessed 10 December 2021).

Rosanna Ayton

As Personal Tutoring Manager at King's College London, Rosanna Ayton supports personal tutors across the whole university through developing resources, delivering training and making connections between faculties and central services to enable effective delivery. Rosanna leads the strategic development of personal tutoring, looking at system, process and policy improvements, and delivers work supporting the university students' mental health and well-being and inclusive education agendas in this area.

Morag Walling

Morag Walling is based at King's College London but employed by The Careers Group, University of London. Her role is to support academic staff and the wider institution to better understand the topics of employability and careers. The aim of this work is to develop sustainable institutional solutions that will enable all students to maximise the value of their academic and King's-wide experience for their future. As a careers and employability professional having worked with young people and graduates from secondary through to tertiary education and beyond, Morag has taken a particular interest in developing an understanding of why many young people find it difficult to relate to these topics.

Case study 3
A data-focused approach to personalising central support programmes and complementing personal tutoring

Alexandra Banks

Themes	Page number locations in the companion book
Data analytics	92–5
Developing a sense of belonging among students	13
Differentiating by individual student needs	108–14
Supplementary support for personal tutoring and advising	22
Supporting student populations	75–85
Transition	105–8

Introduction

Solent University is a vocational institution with 10,000 students and has a focus on equality, diversity and inclusivity. The university champions widening participation and to reinforce this, in 2016, set up a Student Achievement Team. I was appointed as Student Achievement

Manager with a brief to improve retention. Improving retention was relevant to the university's strategic plan 2015–20 and its Access and Participation plan.

Understanding student retention

My first steps were to understand the retention landscape, so I completed a literature review of retention in higher education and began investigating the issues specifically relevant to Solent. A key piece of research was *What Works? Student Retention and Success* (Thomas, 2012; Thomas et al, 2017). Findings included that 8 per cent of students in UK higher education withdraw during their first year and a third of students consider withdrawing. Another key finding was that developing a sense of belonging, where students feel part of their university through the relationships they establish with staff and peers, was critical to retention. Research suggested that the most effective way to improve retention is timely identification of problems and swift action (Cole et al, 2015). Initial data analyses at Solent suggested that retention was closely linked to achievement. Academic failure, such as having to repeat a level, often preceded withdrawal. There were groups of students who each year had higher rates of withdrawal and the reasons declared for withdrawing revealed a complex picture of academic concerns, feelings of isolation, worries about achieving future aspirations and poor academic performance together with financial concerns and personal issues. These findings were consistent with sector findings (Foster et al, 2012; Davies and Elias, 2013).

Developing a retention strategy

Retention emerged as a complex, multidimensional problem and therefore I recognised that the strategy would need to be similarly multi-faceted. The approach was designed to be proactive and reduce risk, formalising the use of data and developing an overarching perspective focusing on prevention rather than cure. I consulted widely across the university with teaching and professional services staff by attending team meetings and leading discussions about retention, resulting in a 'Retention Framework' with four strands of action as follows.

- Developing a suite of live reports to build a picture of three-year trends in retention to understand risk factors and profiles of successful students in terms of background characteristics, engagement and entry qualifications. This also allows me to provide data and expertise for personal tutors to inform their retention work.

- Delivering proactive, targeted programmes of support designed to meet the needs of 'at risk' students (i.e. those groups our data show are at more risk of withdrawing) and working collaboratively with personal tutors to facilitate student success.

- Actively engaging students from the outset and setting high expectations so that they understand their responsibilities. Encouraging a sense of belonging through the meaningful relationships they develop with peers, personal tutors and professional support staff (O'Keefe, 2013; Tate and Hopkins, 2013).

- Organising a cross-university 'Retention Working Group' to gain the overview of retention work, exchange good practice and promote collaborative working. This proved to be key in contributing to the development of a culture of retention and adding value to wider retention and achievement work across the university, together with raising the retention agenda as a shared responsibility (Roberts, 2018).

The strategy's success was dependent on its implementation and, as a strategic priority, it was championed from the top down with a formal reporting line established. I delivered a programme of activities for staff including sharing good practice workshops, such as how to develop a sense of belonging at course level, monthly Twitter discussions and retention conferences. These activities continue and are crucial to maintaining an institutional focus on retention.

Student achievement interventions

The student-facing Achievement Team deliver interventions to support groups of students identified as 'at risk'. These are planned programmes of activities targeted to meet the needs of groups of students with activities throughout the year. Activities include phone calls, individual meetings, seminars, workshops and emails providing information and advice. Each programme provides both generic and personalised support in recognition of both the similar needs of the group and individual circumstances.

Interventions are offered to students repeating modules, resitting assessments, perceived to be 'at risk' by their personal tutors and students returning from a period of suspending their studies. Support is also offered to students in their final year in the form of a 'Student Achievement Tutorial' where their individual student record is discussed together with their desired degree outcome and an action plan for the final months of study is agreed. To maximise the effectiveness of an intervention, personal tutors need to be involved so they can provide subject-specific information and support.

Interventions have proved an effective way of organising support, using resources efficiently and delivering high-quality interactions, while my team have developed considerable expertise in delivering targeted support. The proactive approach with advisors contacting students was innovative at the outset. Student feedback reveals that students do not always recognise when they could benefit from support. If they do recognise that they are at a point in their learner journey when they could benefit from personalised advice, there are varied reasons why they may not come forward, such as being fearful of seeking support or feeling embarrassed. Over time, interventions have evolved, increasingly informed by student feedback. The definition of 'at risk' has broadened and includes 'at a transition point', such as progressing to the next year.

All students may require an intervention at some point and may be contacted under different interventions. Being contacted by the Achievement Team is the norm and part of the support we offer as a university. The team promote their service at Freshers' Fair, pop-up activities and we are present on social media every week to raise our profile.

The 'Academic Referral' intervention involves personal tutors referring students they have any concerns about, which is often before engagement data indicates an issue. It is therefore important that personal tutors understand how student services deliver support for learning and how this complements personal tutoring so they can make better judgements about when to refer students, resulting in more timely support being accessed.

Personal tutor participation in collaborative meetings is effective, an efficient use of time and avoids the student needing to attend multiple meetings. For example, students whose academic record suggests that they may be on track to achieve a degree without honours are invited to attend a meeting with their personal tutor and an achievement advisor. The personal tutor can offer subject-specific advice on building a portfolio of experience to mitigate this outcome and the advisor can explain the academic options available.

More recently, supporting student achievement has included developing learning analytics at Solent. A student's personal engagement data can inform a meeting with the student and enhance the quality of support offered (Rienties et al, 2016). I have reconceptualised the retention question from 'Why are they dropping out?' to 'Why are they not achieving?'

Demonstrating impact

At the end of the first year of implementation in 2017, I completed an impact analysis for each intervention, measured by percentage improvement in retention, progression and/or achievement. There was:

- an 11 per cent higher achievement rate for students who received support while retaking assessments compared to those retaking who did not receive support;

- a 9 per cent improvement in achievement/progression of students returning from having suspended their studies;

- a 14 per cent reduction in the withdrawal rate of repeat-level students;

- a 3 per cent increase in students achieving a first-class degree;

- a 100 per cent student satisfaction rate for the 'academic referral' programme;

- a 12 per cent improvement in the average recorded student attendance.

While it is not possible to prove causality, the 2018–20 impact measures have shown year-on-year improvements in retention for groups targeted with interventions and in five years the non-continuation rate at Solent has improved so that it is consistently better than our benchmark.

Lessons learnt over five years

During the past five years, several features critical to the success of retention have emerged. There is a danger that by having a Student Achievement Team there can be a perception that retention is being dealt with 'by someone else', when in reality retention is everyone's responsibility and all staff have an important role to play. Crucially, the Student Achievement Team have embedded their role by complementing and enhancing the work of personal tutors.

Fundamental to the success of the strategy was raising the retention agenda. This meant developing an institutional understanding that the quality of teaching, learning and assessment, together with support for learning and the overarching student experience, will all impact on retention. To make the strategy sustainable I worked collaboratively with other managers to align the retention framework to the Learning and Teaching Strategy.

I have also learnt the importance of critical reflection and continuous improvement, including balancing impact with cost effectiveness. If an intervention has resulted in an improvement in retention and achievement for a group of students but has required a disproportionate amount of advisor resource, this has been reviewed and redressed.

I learnt that embedding interventions and a culture of retention takes time and so each year I maintain the focus on staff development activities. At the same time, aligning change to the institutional context is more successful than approaching retention as an additional task. Data was more powerful than I expected both as a driver for staff to actively engage with the problem and as a tool to enable a small team to have an impact on large numbers of students. Being able to explore data is essential to develop a sophisticated picture of retention and by establishing three-year trends resource is not wasted actioning 'blips'. My use of data has evolved and impact analyses now include effectiveness by ethnicity and gender, further informing the development of interventions. Data has become an objective and non-judgemental tool for change.

Critical reflections

1. How much influence do you think we, as personal tutors, can have on retention and why? How can you build effective, collaborative working partnerships between different stakeholders who support students, for example, teachers, personal tutors and professional service roles?

2. How effectively is data used to inform timely and targeted student support? How could the data be harnessed more effectively?

3. Do you have a consistent approach across provision to identify students at risk of not achieving? What are the barriers and solutions to making this more effective? What do you think may be some of the drawbacks of labelling students 'at risk'?

References

Cole, C, Coley, T and Lynch-Holmes, K (2015) *Retention and Student Success: Implementing Strategies That Make a Difference*. White Paper Series. Fairfax, VA: Ellican.

Davies, R and Elias, P (2013) *Dropping Out: A Study of Early Leavers from Higher Education*. Department for Education and Skills. [online] Available at: https://warwick.ac.uk/fac/soc/ier/publications/2002/davies_and_elias_2002_rr386.pdf (accessed 10 December 2021).

Foster, E, Lawther, S, Keenan, C, Bates, N, Colley, B and Lefever, R (2012) Higher Education Retention and Engagement Project. [online] Available at: www.advance-he.ac.uk/knowledge-hub/here-project-0 (accessed 10 December 2021).

O'Keefe, P (2013) A Sense of Belonging: Improving Student Retention. *College Student Journal*, 47(4): 605–13.

Rienties, B, Woodthorpe, J, Boroowa, A, Cross, S, Farrington-Flint, L, Herodotou, C, Prescott, L, Mayles, K, Olney, T and Toetenel, L (2016) Reviewing Three Case Studies of Learning Analytics Interventions at the Open University UK. [online] Available at: www.researchgate.net/publication/301591334_Reviewing_three_case-studies_of_learning_analytics_interventions_at_the_open_university_UK (accessed 10 December 2021).

Roberts, J (2018) Professional Staff Contributions to Student Retention and Success in Higher Education. *Journal of Higher Education Policy and Management*, 40(2): 140–53.

Tate, S and Hopkins, P (2013) Re-thinking Undergraduate Students' Transitions to, Through and Out of University. [online] Available at: www.heacademy.ac.uk/system/files/resources/gees_10_transitions_resource_tateandhopkins.pdf (accessed 10 December 2021).

Thomas, L (2012) *Building Student Engagement and Belonging in Higher Education at a Time of Change. Final Report from the What Works? Student Retention and Success Programme.* [online] Available at: www.heacademy.ac.uk/sites/default/files/resources/What_works_final_report.pdf (accessed 10 December 2021).

Thomas, L, Hill, M, O'Mahony, J and Yorke, M (2017) *Supporting Student Success: Strategies for Institutional Change. What Works? Student Retention and Success Programme. Final Report.* [online] Available at: www.advance-he.ac.uk/knowledge-hub/supporting-student-success-strategies-institutional-change (accessed 10 October 2021).

Alexandra Banks

Alexandra Banks is Deputy Head of Student Experience (Achievement) at Solent University. She completed her BSc (Hons) degree in Psychology at the University of Southampton, her PGCE (FE) at Cardiff University and MA in Professional Practice at Solent. She worked in further education for 19 years as a psychology teacher and Director of Teaching and Learning. Since joining Solent she has led on retention and achievement activities, including work to reduce the BAME attainment gap. She is a Higher Education Academy Senior Fellow.

Case study 4
Making belonging explicit by design

Elaine Brown

Themes	Page number locations in the companion book
Coaching	15–21, 136–52
Developing a sense of belonging among students	13
Differentiating by individual student needs	108–14
Experiential design	158–9
Group personal tutoring and advising	108–17
Institutional review and implementation	23–5
Student engagement	44, 56, 57, 58–60, 66–7
Student involvement and co-creation	61, 107, 116, 167–8

Introduction

This case study describes the application of User Experience Design (UXD) based philosophy and tools to implement a model of personal development tutoring (PDT) to improve student outcomes. This approach is unusual because we customarily implement personal tutoring from a service perspective which asks what we can deliver; in contrast, UXD prompts us to ask 'how does this feel?'

Context

Sector context

The continuation of students in higher education is not just an internal, institutional and moral imperative, but an external metric by which higher education institutions are judged (DfE, 2017; Pearce, 2019). Within a context of widening participation, publication of the influential *What Works?* report examined strategies for institutions to improve the retention and success of students and underscored the criticality of student belonging to mitigate the problematised leaving of higher education (Thomas, 2012).

Defined as '*relatedness or connectedness to the institution*' (Thomas, 2012, p 12), descriptions of belonging also include feelings of being accepted, valued and supported (Goodenow, 1993; Strayhorn, 2012; Tinto, 2017). These feelings of belonging are associated with engagement with the institution, specifically here engagement through personal tutoring. Personal tutoring supports a sense of belonging (Yale, 2019) through relationships with staff (Thomas, 2012) and contributes significantly to retention (Grey and Osborne, 2018). Personal tutoring is, however, not just a system of support processes – the ways in which personal tutoring is experienced also matter (Thomas, 2012; Yale, 2019).

Institutional context

Following the publication of *Supporting Student Success: Strategies for Institutional Change* (Thomas et al, 2017), the student retention workstream of Anglia Ruskin University (a post-1992 university) undertook a review of personal tutoring provision that included the literature, good practice across the sector, and our own practice. This review resulted in the proposal of an institution-wide model of PDT (Taylor et al, 2018) that aimed to improve the experience of students by creating relationships so that '*both students and staff... feel valued and supported*' (Taylor et al, 2018, p 7). PDT was rolled out across the institution to first-year undergraduate students in September 2019, to second-year undergraduate students in September 2020, and to third-year undergraduates in September 2021.

Personal development tutoring

User Experience Design

Evolving from human–computer interaction (HCI) and used in the design of software interfaces, User Experience Design is both a philosophy and set of design tools centred on the subjective experiences of interactions with software rather than the functions of software itself. In this context, user experience is defined as a '*person's perceptions and responses resulting from the use and/or anticipated use of a product, system or service*' (ISO, 2010), the design of which aims to create '*outstanding quality experiences*' (Hassenzahl and Tractinsky, 2006, p 95).

Experiential outcomes of personal development tutoring

In the design of PDT, the experiences of students and tutors with existing practices of personal tutoring were explored through interviews, focus groups and analysis of documents such as student-led award nominations. Such experiences made explicit both the 'pain points' and 'moments of delight' experienced by students and tutors.

Taylor et al (2018) found that students approached their personal tutor only when they were experiencing a problem, expecting both empathy and a solution. Perceiving tutee–tutor interaction in this way reduces it to a transaction where the academic tutor is framed in the familiar role of expert and the student acquiesces their agency. Seen through this lens, personal tutoring can be framed as a service (Pine and Gilmore, 1998).

The perception of personal tutoring as a service is not unusual (for example, Yale, 2019; Stuart et al, 2021). Indeed, there are benefits to a service approach to personal tutoring, such as a systematic structure and reassuring outcomes for the institution that can be audited and reported (Tinto, 2017). However, this framing as problem solving situates students in a position of need, in deficit, and is counter to the positive, proactive engagement with tutors that we envisioned for PDT. The community and belonging aspects of PDT are not objective outputs of service but subjective perceptions of experience – students and tutors *feel* valued and supported. Constructively aligning outcomes with design meant adopting an experiential lens, for which we thought UXD would provide insight.

Design for meaning

Hassenzahl (2010) argues that UXD offers a holistic perspective through a hierarchy of three types of goal: *be*-goals, *do*-goals and *motor*-goals – the 'why', 'what' and 'how' of interactions. A service approach typically focuses on the 'what' and the 'how', leaving the 'why' overlooked (Hassenzahl, 2010).

Our meaning, our 'why', are feelings of belonging. Belongingness is a psychological need (Sheldon et al, 2001) and while the experience of belonging is subjective (and therefore experienced in different ways), Hassenzahl (2010) argues that a common core to experiences makes design possible.

Eliciting this common core meant approaching design by asking how students would feel valued and 'seen' through each interaction rather than identifying the procedural or learning outcomes each interaction would achieve. For example, implementing PDT required timetabled group tutorials to create learning communities (the 'what') through discussions and activities (the 'how'). However, without the 'why' to feel valued and 'seen', these learning communities risked defaulting to just another group tutorial.

The design of sessions made explicit opportunities for students to experience being valued and 'seen'. The structure of learning communities suggested ways for personal development tutors to facilitate community and encourage authentic participation through 'check-ins' ('what is going on for you today?') and negotiated ground rules for the group. Similarly, these student experience *be*-goals framed the preparation of personal development tutorials, as personal development tutors checked the student's record for a photograph (to recognise their tutee), engagement data (to ask how study was going) or notes of a previous tutorial (to 'catch up').

Additionally, the way in which these interactions are experienced matters (Thomas, 2012; Yale, 2019). Personal development tutors were supported to enhance their skills and confidence through a suite of continuing professional development (CPD) that included coaching approaches to authentic conversations, scope of the role, familiarisation with resources and processes of referral.

Make value explicit

Using the lens of UXD to make belonging explicit throughout the eco-system of PDT contributed to the success of this approach. Use of this design philosophy enabled us to ask how an interaction would be experienced. Such questioning meant the experiential outcomes of feeling valued and supported, belonging and community could be normalised in conversations alongside institutional and operational outcomes.

Consistent with the iterative design process of UXD, the stories of students' and tutors' experiences of the rollout of PDT were elicited through surveys and follow-up interviews (and the model of PDT was adjusted).

Table 4.1 *The 'what' and 'how' of making belonging explicit in three domains: the overall scheme, students and tutors*

Personal development tutoring (PDT)	Students	Personal development tutors
• institutional focus on community and belonging • institutional conversations highlighting the strategic importance PDT and the positive regard for the role of personal development tutor • explicit structure designed for a consistent student experience • clear communication of expectations • learning communities integrated within the course timetable signalling its equivalence	• prepare for personal development tutorials by prompting recollection: ○ look up photos to 'recognise' the student; ○ greet the student by their name; ○ use engagement dashboards, without judgement, to inform individual personal development tutorials (for example, attendance, grade trend). • use a coaching approach in individual and group sessions to:	• clearly defined role, responsibilities and scope • governance to oversee and protect the scope of the role and receive feedback • time allowance • CPD • community of PDT leaders • a focus on experiential outcomes enabled institutional conversations to ask how the role could be eased of procedural burdens to enable focus on building relationships and community

→

Table 4.1 (Cont.)

Personal development tutoring (PDT)	Students	Personal development tutors
• resources focused on building community rather than delivery (the 'why', the *be*-goal) • an institutional lead and community of faculty leads signalling support for the system of PDT	° listen, rather than solve 'problems' to encourage proactive interaction; ° open discussions; ° plan for the student's own goals (and not the tutor's). • resources focused on activities • reaching out to individuals personally at regular intervals	• joint ownership of institutional resources and flexibility to tailor such resources to fit the context of their community • feedback from students • feedback from tutors

Conclusion

The structure and clarity of student-centred personal tutoring as a service can offer efficiency and measurement; however, it can also miss the point. The use of UXD both as a philosophy and a method places the student and tutor at the heart of a process that constructively aligns the design of PDT with its envisioned experiential outcomes.

Support for personal development tutors included professional development activities that articulated a clear, student-centred rationale. These development activities rehearsed associated behaviours (a professional skillset) to enable students to discover and articulate their own solutions. Academics familiar with the role of 'expert' may also need support to be able to reflect upon a system of 'delivering' tutorials in favour of a more authentic, accessible and discursive community of learning that facilitates envisioned experiential outcomes.

Key messages

- Be clear about the experiential outcome (the 'why') and foreground discussions with this outcome. Any change to the system should enhance the experiential outcome.

- Involve users in the UXD design process (here both students and tutors).

- When evaluating, include qualitative expressions of the experiential outcomes for which you have designed. With appropriate permissions, evaluation reports can include experiential quotes alongside quantitative metrics to normalise their use.

> • Avoid being an individual 'hero' designer and seek feedback on the experiences of students and tutors to iterate the model; each model of PDT is simply another hypothesis.

Critical reflections

1. How do you feel about being a personal tutor at your institution? How do you think your students feel about engaging with personal tutoring? What could improve to help both feel better?

2. To what extent does your institution involve personal tutors and their students in the design of personal tutoring? Describe one way you could positively influence this.

3. Explain two ways in which you as an individual and the personal tutoring system you work within could move from being 'reactive' to student needs to more 'proactive'.

References

Department for Education (2017) *Teaching Excellence and Student Outcomes Framework Specification*. [online] Available at: https://assets.publishing.service.gov.uk/government/uploads/system/uploads/attachment_data/file/658490/Teaching_Excellence_and_Student_Outcomes_Framework_Specification.pdf (accessed 10 December 2021).

Goodenow, C (1993) Classroom Belonging Among Early Adolescent Students: Relationships to Motivation and Achievement. *The Journal of Early Adolescence*, 13(1): 21–43.

Grey, D and Osborne, C (2018) Perceptions and Principles of Personal Tutoring. *Journal of Further and Higher Education*, 44(3): 285–99.

Hassenzahl, M (2010) *Experience Design: Technology for All the Right Reasons*. San Rafael, CA: Morgan and Claypool Publishers.

Hassenzahl, M and Tractinsky, N (2006) User Experience – A Research Agenda. *Behaviour and Information Technology*, 25(2): 91–7.

International Organisation for Standardisation (2010) *Ergonomics of Human-system Interaction – Part 210: Human-centred Design for Interactive Systems*. ISO 9241-210:2010.

Pearce, S (2019) *Independent Review of the Teaching Excellence and Student Outcomes Framework (TEF): Report to the Secretary of State for Education*. [online] Available at: https://assets.publishing.service.gov.uk/government/uploads/system/uploads/attachment_data/file/952754/TEF_Independent_review_report.pdf (accessed 18 December 2021).

Pine, B J and Gilmore, H (1998) Welcome to the Experience Economy. *Harvard Business Review*, 76(4): 97–105.

Sheldon, K M, Elliott, A J, Kim, Y and Kasser, T (2001) What is Satisfying About Satisfying Events? Testing 10 Candidate Psychological Needs. *Journal of Personality and Social Psychology*, 80(2): 325–39.

Strayhorn, T L (2012) *College Students' Sense of Belonging: A Key to Educational Success for all Students*. New York: Routledge.

Stuart, K, Willcocks, K and Browning, R (2021) Questioning Personal Tutoring in Higher Education: An Activity Theoretical Action Research Study. *Educational Action Research*, 29(1): 79–98.

Taylor, R, Hale, E and Khan, K (2018) *Personal Tutor Review: A Report of the Final Outcomes for the Personal Tutor Review*. Internal publication.

Thomas, L (2012) *Building Student Engagement and Belonging in Higher Education at a Time of Change. Final Report from the What Works? Student Retention and Success Programme.* [online] Available at: www.heacademy.ac.uk/sites/default/files/resources/What_works_final_report.pdf (accessed 10 December 2021).

Thomas, L, Hill, M, O'Mahony, J and Yorke, M (2017) *Supporting Student Success: Strategies for Institutional Change. What Works? Student Retention and Success Programme. Final Report.* [online] Available at: www.advance-he.ac.uk/knowledge-hub/supporting-student-success-strategies-institutional-change (accessed 10 October 2021).

Tinto, V (2017) Reflections on Student Persistence. *Student Success*, 8(2): 1–8.

Yale, A T (2019) The Personal Tutor–Student Relationship: Student Expectations and Experiences of Personal Tutoring in Higher Education. *Journal of Further and Higher Education*, 43(4): 533–44.

Elaine Brown

Elaine Brown was previously an academic lecturer in User Experience Design, Director of Studies and then Acting Deputy Dean (Student Experience) in the Faculty of Science and Engineering. She continues her passion for experience design and its applicability to interdisciplinary education through her role as Institutional Lead for Personal Development Tutoring and Ruskin Modules within Anglia Learning and Teaching. Elaine's curiosity to map experience extends to her research using a phenomenographic approach and photo elicitation to explore experiences of belonging for first-year students.

Case study 5

Dissonant discourses: constructing a consistent personal tutoring experience across the whole university

Elaine Brown and Liz Thomas

Themes	Page number locations in the companion book
Coaching	15–21, 136–52
Embedded into teaching	22
Group personal tutoring and advising	108–17
Role definition	12–14
Role types – expert versus generalist; senior and specialised personal tutor and advisor	22–3
Training/Professional development	167–71
Whole-institution approach	24

Contextual overview: personal development tutoring

Our case study examines how one university sought to develop a whole-institution approach to personal tutoring to create a more consistent experience for students, and some of the challenges experienced. The university is regionally rooted having an international reach with 23,500 students. In 2018, the university wanted to improve personal tutoring for undergraduate students to enhance the student experience, improve outcomes in higher education, develop graduate capitals and increase progression to graduate employment or further study. We have not named the university to preserve anonymity; in this case study we refer to institutional documents, which are in the public domain, but we have not referenced them to preserve the identity of the university.

After undertaking institutional research that involved an appreciative inquiry of existing personal tutoring practice both within the university and across the literature, the university developed and implemented the personal development tutoring model, which takes a holistic, student-centred approach. This can be understood as a whole-institution approach (WIA) (Thomas, 2017), and has a number of features: it works across the student lifecycle, encompasses the wider student experience, involves all staff and services and benefits all students. A WIA offers a consistently good experience for students throughout their higher education journey, irrespective of factors such as discipline, campus or mode of study. Implementing a WIA requires appropriate institutional commitment and leadership. It also requires a 'top-down, bottom-up' approach to change (Kift, 2009) which develops the disposition and capacity of staff to engage, changes the institutional structures that facilitate engagement, needs co-ordination and should make use of data and evidence (Thomas, 2017).

The PDT model seeks to develop and support students academically, pastorally and professionally. It utilises an embedded curricular model, offering both one-to-one and group sessions to enable all students to be 'successful'; however, this is defined by individuals. PDT is informed by a coaching model (Lochtie et al, 2018), designed to enable all students to identify and work towards their goals, and to access support and resources from across the university as required.

Coaching for student success training

Prior to the start of the 2019–20 academic year, 'coaching for student success' training was provided for all personal tutors across the university; in total, 22 workshops were delivered between July and October, involving 339 tutors. Each session was co-facilitated by two qualified coaches from an external specialist organisation (with over 13 years' experience in coaching and leadership development); the sessions introduced participants to what 'great' coaching is, the skills needed to be an effective coach, a range of coaching tools and techniques, and opportunities to practise the role and build confidence.

We evaluated the training through surveys with both quantitative and qualitative data. However, we do not have ethical approval to share this data and we therefore offer our personal reflections. The training received a mixed reception. We observed that the majority of staff engaged and felt they benefitted from the training: they learnt about specific tools and developed new skills that they could utilise in their role as personal development tutors. We perceived that some staff felt the training was too generic: it did not recognise their skills and they would have benefitted from more specific training. Some of the more critical staff felt that the training content was 'too obvious', or even a waste of their time, as tutoring is straightforward and unchallenging.

Competing discourses about 'personal tutoring'

As passionate advocates of a more inclusive and proactive tutoring model that utilises coaching to help all students to identify their own goals and work towards them, and overcome any challenges that arise, we were a little disappointed with the reactions to the training. Through discussion about and reflection on the training and the feedback, we realised that the role of a personal (development) tutor within the university – and many others – is open to interpretation and full of contradictions (Stephen et al, 2008; McFarlane, 2016).

Institutional committees, managers, staff and students have different interpretations of the role, and unless these dissonant discourses are exposed and examined, the contribution of personal tutoring to student experience within the institutional framework is unclear, and there will never be a WIA or a consistent student experience. Through our reflection we identified multiple contradictory 'discourses' or beliefs about personal tutoring. Here we identify and explore two competing or dissonant discourses about the role of PDT, and the attributes of an effective tutor.

- The role of personal tutors – support versus success: support for students in need, or the development of success for all students.

- The attributes of an effective tutor – expert versus generalist: tutors are experts and require specialist skills (Lochtie et al, 2018; UKAT, 2019), or all academic staff can be tutors as it is a generalist role and no particular training is required.

Support versus success

The dichotomy between support and success gets to the heart of the problem: is the role of a personal tutor to prevent students who are at risk of withdrawing from higher education from doing so, or to promote the success (however that is defined) of all students?

Personal tutoring has frequently been understood within the university and across the higher education sector as a way of helping students who are at risk of withdrawing to overcome academic and personal problems in order to remain in higher education (Wheeler and Birtle, 1993; Owen, 2002). An earlier discourse at the university positioned personal tutors as *'assisting and facilitating students on any issue relating to their studies'* and having a *'positive impact on student retention'* (taken from an institutional report on personal tutoring from 2011). In contrast, the current 'official' institutional discourse, drawn from strategy documents, has a very different feel to it, with a focus on development and 'success'. The overarching university strategy states a commitment to working with students and the Students' Union to *'create a learning community which encourages active student learning, engagement, and ultimately success'*. The subsidiary Education Strategy has 14 references to success, and only one reference to retention, and the personal development tutor system is framed as developing learning communities and building social capital, and enabling students to self-assess their progress, success and areas for development. While the PDT system is also described as *'supporting student success'* in the Education Strategy, the university's official discourse about personal tutoring is much more about empowering all students to succeed than supporting students with problems to be retained.

But what view do staff subscribe to? It seems that the majority of staff who attended the training understood and embraced the role of the personal development tutor in a similar way to the current official institutional discourse. These staff were seen to welcome the coaching training as it gave them new ideas, skills and tools to use with students. Some also developed personal goals and identified areas for development for themselves. Some experienced the session as an opportunity to learn from each other and share and develop practice. Other staff appeared dissatisfied with the training; they seemed resistant to the new discourse and (perhaps) retained the discourse of 'support'. This group fell into at least two camps: those who felt no training was needed and those who felt more advanced training was required. Those staff who felt no training was needed felt the role was unchallenging, and tended to focus on perceived structural problems within the institution. Conversely, some of the staff appeared concerned about dealing with difficult situations and 'challenging students', and wanted more advanced training. While these are legitimate concerns, they were not the focus of the coaching training.

Expert versus generalist

The second dichotomy is about whether personal tutors need specialist skills or whether all staff can be personal tutors without training (beyond knowing where to signpost students to). The staff who seemed positive about the training, and some who wanted more advanced training (for example, to develop employability goals and graduate capitals), saw the need for a specialist skill set (see for example, *UKAT Professional Development Framework* [UKAT, 2019]). Conversely some staff appeared to feel that specialist skills were not required. This dichotomy may be related to the perceived role of personal tutors, but perhaps also to people's own experience of being tutored as undergraduate students themselves.

Implication of the dissonant discourses

The lack of clarity about the role of personal development tutors and the skills required fed into dissatisfaction with the training and negative feedback. While the university's current discourse on the role of personal tutors appears clear and consistent, it did not seem to be owned by all staff. The training became a site of resistance, with some of the discussion focused on questioning the tutoring approach being adopted by the university, the content of the training and the allocation of resources to the sessions. This is at least in part because the training was experienced as 'top-down'.

This training was delivered quickly to enable staff to operate effectively as personal development tutors from the beginning of the academic year. More effort could have been devoted to developing an appreciation of the reasons and anticipated benefits of the new model of personal development tutoring, to promote ownership. Time could also have been given to exploring different conceptualisations of personal tutoring and the skills involved, to enable a shared interpretation to be forged collaboratively, and to douse the disruptive influence of dissonant discourses.

Shifting the institutional discourse takes time and care needs to be taken to ensure it is not experienced as a top-down takeover. Staff development and 'cultural change' need to be supported and reinforced by institutional structures that reflect the new discourse and provide resources to facilitate change. Training also needs to recognise differential levels of expertise within the staff body, both drawing on this, and, perhaps, letting staff select which level of training they undertake (see for example, Vidaček-Hainš et al, 2011). Without staff buy-in to the institutional discourse, a WIA cannot be achieved.

Critical reflections

1. How do you feel about a 'whole-institution approach' to personal tutoring? Would it improve the student experience and how? How might it potentially hinder improvement for the students and why?

2. On a continuum scale from 1 to 10:

   a. where do you feel the focus of the personal tutor should be on the following two scales:

   - support (#1) versus success (#10)?
   - expert (#1) versus generalist (#10)?

   Describe why you feel this for both scales.

   b. where is your institution's focus for the personal tutor on the following two scales:

   - support (#1) versus success (#10)?
   - expert (#1) versus generalist (#10)?

   Describe why you feel this for both scales.

3. The case study states that student success is defined by individuals.

   a. How would you define student success?

   b. How do you think your students may define their success?

   c. How do you feel your faculty or institution would define student success?

   Identify one potential conflict in these definitions and how you or your institution might overcome it.

References

Kift, S M (2009) *Articulating a Transition Pedagogy to Scaffold and to Enhance the First Year Student Learning Experience in Australian Higher Education*. Final Report for ALTC Senior Fellowship Program. ALTC Resources. [online] Available at: www.altc.edu.au/resource-first-year-learning-experience-kift-2009 (accessed 8 October 2021).

Lochtie, D, McIntosh, E, Stork, A and Walker, B W (2018) *Effective Personal Tutoring in Higher Education*. St Albans: Critical Publishing.

McFarlane, K J (2016) Tutoring the Tutors: Supporting Effective Personal Tutoring. *Active Learning in Higher Education*, 17(1): 77–88.

Owen, M (2002) 'Sometimes You Feel You're in Niche Time': The Personal Tutor System, A Case Study. *Active Learning in Higher Education*, 3(1): 7–23.

Stephen, D E, O'Connell P and Hall, M (2008) 'Going the Extra Mile', 'Fire-fighting', or *Laissez-faire*? Re-evaluating Personal Tutoring Relationships within Mass Higher Education. *Teaching in Higher Education*, 13(4): 449–60.

Thomas, L (2017) *Understanding a Whole Institution Approach to Widening Participation*. Bristol: Office for Fair Access.

UKAT (UK Advising and Tutoring) (2019) The UKAT Professional Framework for Advising and Tutoring. [online] Available at: www.ukat.ac.uk/framework (accessed 1 October 2021).

Vidaček-Hainš, V, Divjak, B and Horvatek, R (2011) Mainstreaming Blended Learning to Enhance the Access, Learning and Retention of Students from Equity Groups. In Thomas, L and Tight, M (eds) *Institutional Transformation to Engage a Diverse Student Body* (pp 327–46). Bingley: Emerald.

Wheeler, S and Birtle, J (1993) *A Handbook for Personal Tutors*. Buckingham: Society for Research into Higher Education and Open University Press.

Elaine Brown

Elaine Brown was previously an academic lecturer in User Experience Design, Director of Studies and then Acting Deputy Dean (Student Experience) in the Faculty of Science and Engineering. She continues her passion for experience design and its applicability to interdisciplinary education through her role as Institutional Lead for Personal Development Tutoring and Ruskin Modules. Elaine's curiosity to map experience extends to her research using a phenomenographic approach and photo elicitation to explore experiences of belonging for first-year students.

Professor Liz Thomas

Liz Thomas is Professor of Higher Education at Edge Hill University; she is interested in widening participation, student experience and institutional change. Her research and related work focus on student engagement and belonging, equitable outcomes for diverse students, and the contribution of learning and teaching. Liz was an expert member of the Teaching Excellence and Student Outcomes Framework (TEF) panel, championing diversity, equity and inclusion. She led the *What Works? Student Retention and Success Programmes*, and has undertaken previous research on personal tutoring and a whole-institution approach to widening participation.

Case study 6
The 'anatomy' of a solutions-focused coaching conversation in personal academic tutoring

Julie De Witt

Themes	Page number locations in the companion book
Careers and employability	122–7
Coaching	15–21, 136–52
Differentiating by individual student needs	108–14
Reflective practice	153–67, 170–1

Introduction

I have a background in medical imaging so understanding the science and what 'lies beneath' is a central tenet of my professional practice. In my higher education practice, understanding how to have better tutoring conversations has led me to achieve an MA in Leadership Coaching and Mentoring. So, utilising a solution-focused coaching approach is central to my practice in personal academic tutoring (PAT) but how and why it works is difficult to explain as conversations happen behind closed doors. I am often asked to give examples so through this case study I hope to explore and 'dissect' how and why this approach works. It is through reflective practice that we gain a better understanding of the conditions for 'quality conversations' (Grant, 2013). The names have been changed and some of the finer detail 'smudged' for confidentiality purposes.

About the conversation

Gemma asked to see me: she had secured an interview for her dream job in a couple of weeks' time; she seemed hesitant. She wanted help to prepare for the interview and for me to ask her some questions. She came along; we had a private office space, I had a list of questions. Her answers were hesitant, unsure, timid. I then asked a problem-solving-type question; these are commonly asked in our professional setting. Tears welled up; she said she didn't know and stated she would never get the job.

This was not how I had envisaged this conversation panning out. Perhaps, as personal tutors, this may resonate. Conversations which one expects to be very straightforward suddenly take a turn; this can be unsettling, difficult and challenging at times.

I could have given platitudes, but that would have been sympathy and that did not feel right. I could have made light of it, we have all made mistakes after all, and told her a funny story about myself but that would have turned the focus on to me and potentially minimised her emotions. I could have tried to avoid this, passed this on to another service (such as Well-being or Careers) and got her out the door, but right then I needed to sit with this discomfort and have the courage to be vulnerable with her. I needed to have this conversation, that was the empathetic thing to do.

So, I leaned into the discomfort I was feeling, staying in this conversation and changing it to a coaching conversation, so she would leave with a plan of her own devising. I remember distinctly putting down the list of questions to signal that the conversation was changing. I placed both my feet on the floor; this grounds me and gives me time to think. I consciously opened my body, faced square on to Gemma and took some breaths. We sat in silence for a moment.

Solutions-focused coaching (SFC) is about finding the exception in the narrative and moving that person towards a solution which they will own (O'Connell et al, 2012). Lochtie et al (2018) note that the defining feature of the solutions-focused approach, as opposed to a cognitive behavioural approach, is that the former focuses on goals and moving forward rather than exploring the problem. Gemma wanted this job and yet she had just said she would never get it; she didn't believe in herself. She didn't know what to do if she found her-self in a situation where she needed to make a difficult decision. I asked if she had found herself in any situations in the past where she was unsure: what had she done, what had helped, who had helped, what had helped reinforce that learning? She tapped almost imme-diately into an example: about how she had asked for help, how someone had supported her, how she had learnt from that and how her confidence had grown. I asked how she could apply that to her current problem. She paused and thought, and then gave me an answer. She still wasn't sure exactly but it was a confident answer, it would be fine in an interview. She smiled and laughed. The rest of the conversation then involved thinking about her action plan to ensure she was well prepared for the interview.

Gemma got the job.

Dissecting the conversation

Reflecting on a conversation such as this, I can start to 'dissect the anatomy' of an SFC approach, as applied to a PAT conversation.

The 'heart' of the conservation centred around building confidence but also my courage to lean into the vulnerability that this role can often throw us into. In my experience, personal tutoring conversations often end up centred around 'enoughness'; this may be a student expressing not being good enough to be at university, as well as not being proficient, quick or confident enough. In this case it was clearly 'good enough' territory that was being expressed. This can be uncomfortable as a tutor; I am not alone in the feeling. Research suggests that a lack of confidence and training in supporting students effectively can result in variable quality of support (McFarlane, 2016; Walker, 2020). I believe that these feelings are actually related to an issue around the culture of scarcity and shame (Brown, 2012). This is complex and in order to understand it I first need to understand the issues from that person's perspective rather than trying to guess or make assumptions. It also means that telling a person what to do or instructing them will not work and is why adopting a solutions-focused coaching approach is my preferred approach.

The 'bones' of this conversation, the foundations, came from using noticing skills and then being able to lean into that uncomfortable silence with empathy and compassion. There is always a temptation to fill this void with advice, sympathy or platitudes. I fight that urge all the time. Sometimes, in conversations, the urge is more to chastise or warn, for example 'why didn't you prepare better?'. I took the time to ground myself, to breathe, to remember this is a conversation of thinking equals (Kline, 2009). This is not about me; the phrase in my head is 'Julie, button it, listen'. In my experience, this is perhaps the most challenging aspect in coaching as a tutor because the expectation is that we will give the answer. Kline (2009) addresses this tension by reminding us that a professional's first job is to create the conditions for people to think and she equates this with creating equality in a thinking environment.

The 'muscles' of this conversation come from the questions that I asked. I needed to find something positive because you cannot coach a problem, only something stated in the positive. I could do this through open questioning, paraphrasing to help reinforce and confirm the responses, and carefully listening to the responses. I was listening to what Gemma was not saying as much as to what she was saying, so was using intuition and coaching presence (Iliffe-Wood, 2014). This is a skill that comes with practice because a frown or slight hesitation in the voice might indicate she was unsure.

Finally, the 'brains' of this conversation come from the action planning that must always emerge in any coaching conversation. A coaching conversation is one which has purpose and ends with deliverable actions which the person is willing to commit to (Hicks, 2013). This is reiterated in Grant and O'Connor's (2018) study in which they confirmed that solution-focused questions were more effective than problem-focused questions but that adding some positive affirmation from action planning was the most effective strategy of all. So, Gemma needed to leave the meeting with some clear actions that she had formulated so she was clear about what she wanted to do next, how she wanted to proceed and if she needed to involve anyone else. This action planning aspect is the part that can get overlooked and yet is crucial in any SFC approach.

I often get asked if it is okay to offer advice. This is a common concern. The solutions the other person generates will always be the best ones for them. Advice will get in the way and may prevent a better solution emerging; this gets to the essence of coaching and its values. I see coaching as a way of being (a mindset), not just as a tool or model. While it is okay to offer advice sometimes, I would always caveat it, offering it as a suggestion only for discussion and remembering that it is fine for the student to discount it.

Learning points for using a solutions-focused approach in personal tutoring

What is provided here is an example. While no two students are the same, you may find the following learning points for using a solutions-focused approach in personal tutoring are transferable to your everyday practice.

- Importantly, coaching by its nature is non-judgemental; this is a non-deficit approach, meaning that the tutor must believe the other person is capable of developing their own solution. This is so they do not 'rush in' and offer the 'answer'.

- It perhaps works best when not linked to a performance management 'problem' because trust between the tutor and student is key.

- A SFC approach has a role to play in developing some graduate attributes such as problem solving, goal setting and autonomy. It may also play a role in addressing equality agendas because the values underpinning coaching are inherently non-judgemental.

- I suggest the coach does not need to be an expert in every situation because the essence of a SFC approach is to facilitate and empower, not 'solve' a problem. Trusting in the process and the use of open questions, giving the person 'time to think' and trusting them to develop their own solutions is truly empowering.

Critical reflections

1. To what extent do you feel you are already using a solution-focused coaching approach with your students? Identify which of the aspects covered in the case study you feel you already employ in conversations with your students and which you would like to start using or use more often.

2. A solution-focused coaching conversation should always end with a future action, no matter how small. Do you currently build action planning time into your one-to-ones and what are the benefits of doing this?

3. In one-to-ones, do you feel more comfortable being the 'expert' and offering advice or being more of a facilitator to help your students create their own solutions? Why do you think you feel this way?

References

Brown, B (2012) *Daring Greatly: How the Courage to be Vulnerable Transforms the Way We Live, Love, Parent, and Lead*. London: Penguin.

Grant, A M (2013) Steps to Solutions: A Process for Putting Solution-focused Coaching Principles into Practice. *The Coaching Psychologist*, 9(1): 36–44.

Grant, A M and O'Connor, S A (2018) Broadening and Building Solution-focused Coaching: Feeling Good is Not Enough. *Coaching: An International Journal of Theory, Research and Practice*, 11(2): 165–85.

Hicks, R F (2013) *Coaching as a Leadership Style: The Art and Science of Coaching Conversations for Healthcare Professionals*. Abingdon: Routledge.

Iliffe-Wood, M (2014) *Coaching Presence: Building Consciousness and Awareness in Coaching Interventions*. London: Kogan Page Publishers.

Kline, N (2009) *More Time to Think: A Way of Being in the World*. Thirsk: Fisher King Publishing.

Lochtie, D, McIntosh, E, Stork, A and Walker, B W (2018) *Effective Personal Tutoring in Higher Education*. St Albans: Critical Publishing.

McFarlane, K J (2016) Tutoring the Tutors: Supporting Effective Personal Tutoring. *Active Learning in Higher Education*, 17(1): 77–88.

O'Connell, B, Palmer, S and Williams, H (2012) *Solutions Focused Coaching in Practice*. London: Routledge.

Walker, B W (2020) Tackling the Personal Tutoring Conundrum: A Qualitative Study on the Impact of Developmental Support for Tutors. *Active Learning in Higher Education*. [online] Available at: https://doi.org/10.1177/1469787420926007 (accessed 14 January 2022).

Julie De Witt

Julie De Witt is a senior lecturer at the University of Derby (UoD), a Senior Fellow of the Higher Education Academy, and a diagnostic radiographer by background. With a special interest in coaching as a pedagogic approach in higher education (and an MAEd in leadership coaching and mentoring), Julie is currently working with colleagues in the Centre of Excellence in Learning and Teaching at UoD on the implementation and evaluation of a coaching approach for personal academic tutoring.

Case study 7
Developing an effective institutional personal tutoring and development framework to support student success

Harriet Dunbar-Morris

Themes	Page number locations in the companion book
Boundaries between roles	53–73
Careers and employability	122–7
Framework of personal tutoring and advising	23–5
Institutional review and implementation	23–5
Pastoral support	21–2, 56
Personal tutor and advisor forums	–
Personal tutoring and advising curriculum	122–8
Training/Professional development	167–71
Role types – expert versus generalist; senior and specialised personal tutor and advisor	22–3

Introduction

The University of Portsmouth is a modern post-1992, multi-disciplinary university with a strong tradition of widening participation and of integrating research, professional practice, and simulated and real-world learning into courses. It offers taught courses at undergraduate and postgraduate level to 23,769 students (2019–20 data). Our university strategy highlights our commitment to personalised academic and pastoral support, focused on well-being and resilience, to enhance every student's experience and outcomes, and to engage every student in a life-changing experience.

In this case study I outline how a new personal tutoring and development framework was developed. I present key principles of the approach designed to provide an effective organisational and structural model of student support. I focus on how the project group developed the framework, and resolved key questions and issues for personal tutoring for the benefit of students and their success.

Scope

The framework was developed iteratively by a group of staff, sabbatical officers and students brought together between January 2019 and May 2020 to develop a new single framework for personal tutoring and personal development planning (PDP), which was approved in June and implemented in September 2020. It replaced two frameworks previously in use at the university and completed the operational annexes of the Curriculum Framework, which had been developed during a large-scale curriculum-revision exercise (Dunbar-Morris et al, 2019). The new framework was required because the University Vision and Strategy (University of Portsmouth, nd) and the Curriculum Framework (University of Portsmouth, 2018) highlighted the need:

- for an excellent student experience for all students;
- for a new personal tutoring and development framework to support Portsmouth students;
- to ensure the delivery of courses that provide the knowledge, skills and attributes for success, as defined in the 'Hallmarks of the Portsmouth Graduate' (a set of graduate attributes).

In order to develop an effective framework to which staff and students would sign up, the project drew on a variety of sources of input. These included:

- outcomes from key projects, sector literature, policies or frameworks, including an Office for Students-funded project 'Raising Awareness Raising Aspirations' (RARA) of which Portsmouth had been a part;
- Portsmouth PDP working group and personal tutor symposium;
- staff and student voices, including sabbatical officers, associate deans, senior tutors, student faculty representatives and course leaders.

Principles

To arrive at the key principles at the heart of our framework it was important to have these both evidence based and community recognised, so we drew on findings from RARA (Basi et al, 2019) and staff and student feedback.

A key issue raised was how our framework would ensure student success. Personal tutoring and its link to student success was described by Liz Thomas in the *What Works? Student Retention and Success Change Programme.*

> *Personal tutors can improve student retention and success in the following ways:*
>
> • *enabling students to develop a relationship with an academic member of staff in their discipline or programme area and feeling more connected;*
>
> • *helping staff get to know students;*
>
> • *providing students with reassurance, guidance and feedback about their academic studies in particular.*
>
> (Thomas, 2012, p 43)

Previously, final-year students had changed from having their personal tutor to their project supervisor as tutor, meaning the relationship that had developed between student and personal tutor was lost. Additionally, some students reported an unhelpful link when the person providing personal support also oversaw a key part of their academic work.

Thus, a key change we agreed in our principles – one we would encourage other institutions to consider in developing their own framework – is that students keep the same personal tutor throughout their course.

Another change was to encourage students to see tutoring differently from how it might have been experienced at school or college – to engage with personal tutoring even if they were not having issues. Our approach is more developmental and provides students with the tools to help themselves, which is at the centre of our approach at Portsmouth: '*My personal tutor has been fantastic and really helped me grow not only academically but personally as well*' (Student, NSS 2020). We therefore included solution-focused coaching (Lochtie et al, 2018, pp 136–52) as an element of personal tutoring.

Alison Stenton of the RARA project summarises both the need to ensure clear boundaries between the role of the tutor and other supporting services, and that good signposting was facilitated by tutors to the services:

> *...the personal tutor needs firm boundaries to lean on and concise, up-to-date resources to support effective signposting to specialist support... readily accessible professional services are essential to complementing personal tutoring systems.*
>
> (Stenton, 2017)

This is another of our key principles which we would recommend to the sector because it enables the tutor to focus on their own areas of expertise and responsibility, and for students to be provided with appropriate support from the relevant services within theirs.

Areas of responsibility for personal tutors

Our framework highlights three key areas in which the personal tutor has a role to play: academic, pastoral and professional development.

One of the students at the RARA conference summarises what we found in our desktop research: the need to ensure personal tutoring is first and foremost seen as part of staff's academic role:

> ...to re-frame personal tutoring as teaching, rather than looking at it as a separate support system provided by the university [but] to merge both the pastoral and academic approach for all personal tutors so that, as universities, we reconceptualise personal tutoring as an academic approach to give all students well-rounded support.
>
> (AlHakim, 2018)

Given the central role and relationship that personal tutors have with students, they are key to ensuring students are enabled to develop employability skills and discuss personal development from an academic standpoint. As the curriculum-revision exercise had embedded the hallmarks within the curriculum, we then ensured tutors were empowered to build on that within our personal tutoring curriculum. Tutors therefore have responsibilities to:

- help students develop graduate attributes;

- encourage students' professional development through engagement with course-related activities.

This change of focus, where personal tutoring is seen as teaching with its own curriculum, is one way we approached issues raised about tutoring being seen as an additional task or more about pastoral support for issues. We would recommend it for consideration by those contemplating developing or reviewing their own framework.

Personal tutor training and development

Having agreed these key areas of responsibility, it was equally important to support personal tutors. While those new to their role might require help with topics to cover, more experienced tutors might require help with content relating to the key themes that we outlined and expected students to have exposure to. These were drawn from Lochtie et al (2018) and included:

- getting to know you;

- getting connected;

- enhancing your future.

We developed an example spiral curriculum to support tutors on undergraduate and postgraduate taught courses in each year, and for a variety of session types (individual, group, online or face-to-face).

For those considering their own tutoring curriculum I will now explain some of our thinking which might be useful in your own developments.

As we wanted to embed employability in personal tutoring, 'enhancing your future' sessions provided students with developing opportunities to practise placement, volunteering and job-finding skills, and get feedback on their developing interview approach using 'shortlist me' (an online tool for interview skills). Sessions also introduced students to the concept of PDP and what the hallmarks represent in addition to how they link with employability. We drew on work from existing projects, such as work undertaken in the Business School to develop a toolkit called 'brand me', which is designed to help students understand and develop personal branding for career success, and employability-related self confidence (Tymon et al, 2020). Covered at several points in the curriculum, it includes students making a series of elevator pitch presentations. Students have described the skills they gained from the series of presentations.

> In my second presentation I look increasingly calm, maintaining eye contact... in the final presentation I could talk confidently about my work experience and skills... doing the 'brand me' videos this year has given me the confidence to sell myself by talking about my skills and how they are relevant to an employer.
>
> I have done quite a few presentations [on placement] and got really good feedback I wouldn't have been able to do a lot of them before doing 'brand me'.
>
> (Tymon et al, 2020, pp 1828–9)

Importantly, a focused training programme and dedicated website, the Personal Tutoring @ UoP website, developed by the RARA project and represented in Figure 7.1, affords tutors the opportunity for personal development, access to up-to-date curriculum resources and the ability to share practices and innovations.

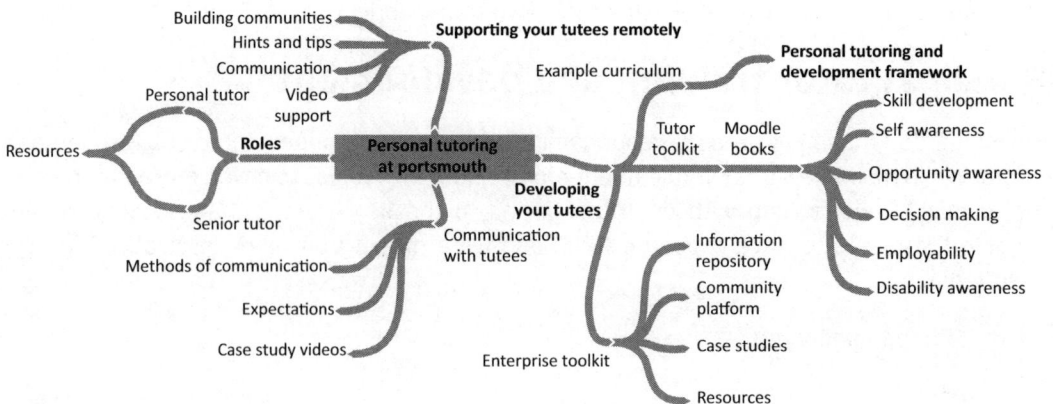

Figure 7.1 *A visual representation of the different elements of the Personal Tutoring @ University of Portsmouth website*

For example, tutors are signposted to sources to help them use solution-focused coaching and encouraged to explore these, with support from senior tutors, and select the approach that best suits them and their students. During the Covid-19 pandemic the role of the personal tutor was paramount. A senior tutor ran a session on meeting the challenge of remote personal tutoring. The session recording and additional resources for tutors on supporting students remotely are available on the Personal Tutoring @ UoP website.

Conclusion

From the work developing the personal tutoring and development framework to ensure personal tutors support student success, we recommend:

- ensuring tutoring is seen as part of teaching with its own curriculum;

- ensuring students keep the same tutor throughout their course;

- providing tutors with access to resources and training to support them to support students to help themselves.

Critical reflections

1. Does anything need to change in your department, faculty or institution for personal tutoring to be reframed as teaching and as an academic approach to give all students well-rounded support?

2. Explain three strategies to encourage students to see their personal tutor even if they have no 'issues'.

3. Within your personal tutoring activity and the processes you work within, where might there be further opportunities to support your students' employability? Describe a small action you could take to move this forward.

References

AlHakim, R (2018) Personal Tutoring is Teaching: A Student Review. [online] Available at: www.raratutor. ac.uk/personal-tutoring-teaching-student-review (accessed 10 December 2021).

Basi, A, Broglia, E, Ayton, R, McKeever, M, Stenton, A and Attenborough, C (2019) *Raising Awareness, Raising Aspiration: Personal Tutors Helping to Tackle Attainment Gaps*. Sheffield: University of Sheffield.

Brand Me Toolkit. [online] Available at: https://rise.articulate.com/share/Cmjz3gjWF3fNCLWTe SOCguc1GWbTqYnr#/lessons/knWuclkbTYWsNROIKU6xuY1_cJdc31vi (accessed 10 December 2021).

Dunbar-Morris, H, Barlow, A and Layer, A (2019) A Co-constructed Curriculum: A Model for Implementing Total Institutional Change in Partnership with Students. *Journal of Educational Innovation Partnership and Change*, 5(1).

Lochtie, D, McIntosh, E, Stork, A and Walker, B W (2018) *Effective Personal Tutoring in Higher Education*. St Albans: Critical Publishing.

Personal Tutoring @UoP (nd). [online] Available at: https://personaltutoring.port.ac.uk/home (accessed 10 December 2021).

Shortlist Me (nd). [online] Available at: https://go.shortlister.com/marketplace/portsmouthuni (accessed 10 December 2021).

Stenton, A (2017) Why Personal Tutoring is Essential for Student Success. [online] Available at: www.heacademy.ac.uk/blog/why-personal-tutoring-essential-student-success (accessed 23 October 2021).

Thomas, L (2012) *Building Student Engagement and Belonging in Higher Education at a Time of Change. Final Report from the What Works? Student Retention and Success Programme.* [online] Available at: www.heacademy.ac.uk/sites/default/files/resources/What_works_final_report.pdf (accessed 10 December 2021).

Tymon, A, Harrison, C and Batistic, S (2020) Sustainable Graduate Employability: An Evaluation of 'Brand Me' Presentations as a Method for Developing Self-confidence. *Studies in Higher Education*, 45(9): 1821–33.

University of Portsmouth (2018) *Curriculum Framework Operational Annexes, June 2018.* [online] Available at: http://policies.docstore.port.ac.uk/policy-237.pdf (accessed 10 December 2021).

University of Portsmouth (2018) *Curriculum Framework Specification, June 2018.* [online] Available at: http://policies.docstore.port.ac.uk/policy-217.pdf (accessed 10 December 2021).

University of Portsmouth (nd) Hallmarks of a Portsmouth Graduate. [online] Available at: www.port.ac.uk/about-us/structure-and-governance/our-people/student-charter-and-graduate-hallmarks (accessed 10 December 2021).

University of Portsmouth (nd) *Personal Tutoring and Development Framework.* [online] Available at: https://drive.google.com/file/d/1nHISPMxaka9al6-s1FKzRylB8FKLIUzS (accessed 10 December 2021).

University of Portsmouth (nd) University Vision 2030 and Strategy 2025. [online] Available at: www.port.ac.uk/about-us/our-ambition/our-strategy (accessed 10 December 2021).

Dr Harriet Dunbar-Morris PFHEA, NTF

As Dean of Learning and Teaching at the University of Portsmouth, Harriet Dunbar-Morris is responsible for providing leadership in the enhancement and evaluation of the student experience. She champions the student voice and facilitates partnership working, ensuring student engagement is central to the university's activities. Harriet has led the revision of the curriculum framework, including embedding the Hallmarks of the Portsmouth Graduate within the curriculum, and developed the personal tutoring and development framework. She undertook research in higher education at the University of Oxford. Post-Oxford, Harriet has held positions at UCAS, the 1994 Group, and the Universities of Bath and Bradford.

Case study 8

How a student and staff partnership informed the co-creation of an online professional development course for personal tutors

Peter Fitch, Alex Standen, Abbie King and Sam Smidt

Themes	Page number locations in the companion book
Differentiating by subject area	–
Institutional review and implementation	23–5
Group personal tutoring and advising	108–17
Reflective practice	153–67, 170–1
Research and evaluation	4, 12, 175–98
Student involvement and co-creation	61, 107, 116, 167–8
Transition	105–8
Training/Professional development	167–71

Background

University College London (UCL) is a multi-disciplinary institution with more than 43,000 students across 11 faculties. In 2016, a review of UCL's personal tutoring provision concluded that, given its size and complexity, a 'one-size-fits-all' approach was not appropriate and that each undergraduate and taught postgraduate programme should decide how best to provide tutoring locally. Programmes should provide access to personal guidance and support relating to academic progress, careers and personal professional development, and general well-being (UCL, 2016). Different models exist, depending on the nature of the programme, cohort size, staffing and students' location.

Personal tutors are expected to engage with institutional training and continuous professional development to support and enhance practice (Grey and Osborne, 2018; Lochtie et al, 2018; McGill et al, 2020). However, workload, emphasis on other aspects of the 'academic' job and limited awareness of, or incentives for engaging with training opportunities can hinder staff engagement with traditional workshops (Dhillon et al, 2008; McFarlane, 2016; Grey and Osborne, 2018; Yale, 2019). Training and development should move away from traditional transactional approaches to longitudinal and cross-institutional opportunities (for example, Lochtie et al, 2018; Walker, 2020a). Lochtie et al (2018) highlight how structured opportunities for reflection with peers supports tutors' development of professional insights, objectivity and confidence as well as helping to reduce stress and anxiety, and in responding to difficult situations.

To review and update UCL's training for personal tutors, we undertook an institutional student partnership project in 2018–19 through UCL's flagship ChangeMakers initiative (Marie, 2018). The project explored staff and student experiences; the findings informed the development of a new asynchronous online course co-created between the student researchers and educational development staff.

This case study discusses the process, findings and areas of applicability to other institutions, namely perceptions of personal tutoring, ideas for developing online content and benefits of student–staff partnership working.

Student-led qualitative research

Three student researchers were supported in running six student focus groups (eight to 12 participants per group) and 11 semi-structured interviews with academic and professional services staff, chosen for their role in organising provision locally and/or being recognised for their commitment to personal tutoring. Questions explored:

- common difficulties;
- whether tutees receive the support they need;
- best practice;
- the guidance and development opportunities tutors need.

The student researchers generated a rich qualitative data set and completed a self-driven thematic analysis, compiling crossover themes that were recommended areas of improvement in personal tutoring. They identified five common themes.

Consistency, regularity and responsiveness

Discussions highlighted considerable variability in engagement from and with personal tutors, linked to uneven awareness and understanding of the role.

Students sought consistency where possible and appropriate. Some preferred regular meetings (weekly, fortnightly), and most recognised the usefulness of knowing specific office hours when they can connect with their personal tutor.

The monitoring and recording of tutee meetings was suggested to be powerful in supporting development of the relationship, setting and tracking goals and writing references.

Location/environment

Students and staff acknowledged the importance of access to space for meetings which facilitated conversation and confidentiality. Students commented that office-based meetings can be intimidating and, in certain circumstances, 'walking meetings' or coffee in communal spaces could be appropriate.

Role clarity and expectations

Providing explicit information for both staff and students to align expectations and help in establishing boundaries was deemed essential.

Students reflected on induction 'information overload', suggesting that key information be (re)flagged in meetings with tutors. Students should be made aware at an early stage of the importance of proactively engaging with personal tutors, who will likely write reference letters.

Staff suggestions included a framework expanding on policy, answers to frequently asked questions and guidance on tracking and discussing students' progress across meetings.

Participants commented that personal tutoring is not just pastoral, highlighting the importance of academic support: this involved discussing practical matters such as module choice and feedback, and connecting with the programme of study and wider discipline (Fung, 2017).

Staff sought clarity on group tutoring and how this should be matched with individual meetings; students expressed a preference for a combination of both.

Motivating student engagement

Students and staff highlighted the need for a reason to engage, particularly with scheduled meetings. Suggestions included tutees completing review forms prior to meetings (establishing an agenda) and action plans to provide continuity between meetings. Locally, students recommended that departments seek targeted feedback to explore students' engagement with, and experience of personal tutoring.

Staff noted that tutee relationships shift as students progress and their circumstances change. Students identified the importance of informal opportunities in interaction for building relationships.

Staff recognition and peer support

Both groups acknowledged the high workload associated with effective personal tutoring. Possible solutions included workload allocation models, local cultures of support utilising additional staff (including professional and technical services) and recognition or reward for personal tutoring (for example the UK Advising and Tutoring's (UKAT) Professional Recognition Scheme: UKAT, 2019; Walker, 2020b). Several participants recommended establishing a community of practice for peer support and guidance.

Co-creating the online course

The students' findings informed the development of a new online course, which is both an asynchronous structured course for new and experienced personal tutors, and a 'one-stop' resource for support on specific areas within our institutional context.

We storyboarded content with the student researchers and digital education colleagues within an agreed sectional structure as follows.

1. Contexts of personal tutoring.
2. Getting started.
3. Building and maintaining a good relationship.
4. Academic support.
5. Pastoral support.
6. Supporting professional development.
7. Remote personal tutoring (incorporated in August–September 2020 in response to the Covid-19 pandemic).
8. Conclusion; staff well-being, further development opportunities.

In order to find effective ways to deliver content, the student researchers analysed feedback from other UCL staff-facing online courses and identified approaches to implement. Short videos, reflective activities and content to encourage (asynchronous) peer engagement were agreed upon.

The student researchers developed videos, checklists, 'top tips', activities and scenarios. Educational development staff drafted sections on boundaries and expectations, coaching approaches to conversations, and supporting assessment and feedback. Content for sections on careers and well-being was developed in collaboration with the relevant UCL teams.

The course was peer reviewed by colleagues from across the university and launched in March 2020.

Impact

As of September 2021, the course had 439 registered users. On average it has over 1000 views per month, with participants making over 300 posts on interactive activities each month. The most viewed elements cover 'the role of a personal tutor' (UK-wide and institutional nuances), ideas for engaging tutees in groups and individually, and department-specific approaches.

Interactive elements inviting reflection and sharing tend to elicit the most engagement. We have responded to this need for peer support by establishing a personal tutoring community through Microsoft Teams.

We have postponed follow-up focus groups because of the Covid-19 pandemic; these will explore staff perspectives and experiences of students whose tutors have completed the training. Eighty per cent of initial participant feedback gives a general experience score of 'good' to 'excellent' (45 per cent 'excellent'). When asked what is good or helpful in the course, staff participants highlighted the following:

- 'pace, structure, variety';
- 'description of the full range of responsibilities';
- 'useful information and reassurance';
- 'a chance to think through experiences and update on what is centrally available';
- 'scenarios as a way of discussing and thinking about issues that might arise'.

When asked what could be improved or developed, the majority of responses requested downloadable summaries and workflows for easy access and personal prompts at a later date.

The online course is successful in providing a single and accessible resource for staff development. Those that completed the online course before attending workshops have flagged its value ahead of discussing scenarios and specific challenges in the synchronous environment. Our initial evaluation aligns with Walker's (2020a) findings where colleagues highlighted the impact of professional development resources in clarifying the role of the personal tutor, exploring different models for student-centred practice (for example, coaching skills) and a developmental nature rooted in realism around complexities of the role and the value of peer support.

Conclusion

Key findings and implications

One of our key findings relates to the benefit of student–staff partnership working: students were active participants in the project, lending their expertise to develop this vital aspect of their university experience. Felten et al (2019) argue that students having greater agency in academic development is a more equitable and inclusive approach in meeting the needs of the whole academic community; it will continue to inform our approach.

Our student-led qualitative research found students and staff valued the following.

- Consistency, regularity and responsive contact to develop and maintain the relationship.

- Explicit information to aid expectation alignment.

- Using review forms and development activities to make meetings meaningful and encourage engagement.

- Acknowledgement of the value of personal tutoring in workload, recognition schemes and communities of practice.

We created a resource that is institution specific, can be accessed at any time and in any order, and can easily be updated to respond to changing staff needs and institutional priorities. We are aware that numerous institutions have, or are developing, their own online courses for personal tutors and hope that sharing our approach and initial participant feedback will be transferable to such developments across the sector.

Next steps

Our approach to personal tutoring staff development aligns with Lochtie et al's (2018) suggestion that it should not occur in isolation from practice and that opportunities for reflection within development workshops and peer communities aids the consolidation and contextualisation of skills and knowledge. Our ongoing enhancement plans include:

- continual review and updates to the online course;

- creating downloadable and accessible resources;

- support for personal tutors in obtaining professional recognition through UKAT's Professional Recognition Scheme and participating in wider sectoral recognition and reward opportunities (UKAT, 2019; Walker, 2020b);

- undertaking a student researcher project to explore the impact of resources on the staff and student experience.

Critical reflections

1. For your own practice, identify two barriers which hinder student–staff partnership working. What solutions can you think of to overcome these?

2. What are the pros and cons of a personal tutoring system which is:

    - 'centralised' and whole institution?

    - 'localised' and devised at course level?

3. Describe what 'effective' peer support could be to enhance your personal tutoring practice. If this isn't already available, what are the next small steps you could take to help initiate it?

References

Dhillon, J K, McGowan, M and Wang, H (2008) How Effective Are Institutional and Departmental Systems of Student Support? Insights from an Investigation into the Support Available to Students at One English University. *Research in Post-Compulsory Education*, 13(3): 281–93.

Felten, P, Abbot, S, Kirkwood, J, Long, A, Lubicz-Nawrocka, T, Mercer-Mapstone, L and Verwood, R (2019) Reimagining the Place of Students in Academic Development. *International Journal for Academic Development*, 24(2): 192–203.

Fung, D (2017) *A Connected Curriculum for Higher Education*. London: UCL Press. [online] Available at: https://discovery.ucl.ac.uk/id/eprint/1558776/1/A-Connected-Curriculum-for-Higher-Education.pdf (accessed 6 October 2021).

Grey, D and Osborne, C (2018) Perceptions and Principles of Personal Tutoring. *Journal of Further and Higher Education*, 44(3): 285–99.

Lochtie, D, McIntosh, E, Stork, A, and Walker, B W (2018) *Effective Personal Tutoring in Higher Education*. St Albans: Critical Publishing.

Marie, J (2018) Students as Partners. In Davies, J P and Pachler, N (eds) *Teaching and Learning in Higher Education: Perspectives from UCL* (pp 35–47). London: UCL IOE Press.

McFarlane, K J (2016) Tutoring the Tutors: Supporting Effective Personal Tutoring. *Active Learning in Higher Education,* 17(1): 77–88.

McGill, C M, Ali, M and Barton, D (2020) Skills and Competencies for Effective Academic Advising and Personal Tutoring. *Frontiers in Education*, 5: 135.

UCL (2016) Personal Tutoring, Guidance and Support for UCL students. [online] Available at: www.ucl.ac.uk/teaching-learning/sites/teaching-learning/files/edcomm_personal_tutoring_guidance_and_support_for_ucl_students.doc (accessed 6 October 2021).

UKAT (UK Advising and Tutoring) (2019) The UKAT Professional Framework for Advising and Tutoring. [online] Available at: www.ukat.ac.uk/framework (accessed 1 October 2021).

Walker, B W (2020a) Tackling the Personal Tutoring Conundrum: A Qualitative Study on the Impact of Developmental Support for Tutors. *Active Learning in Higher Education*. [online] Available at: https://doi.org/10.1177/1469787420926007 (accessed 14 January 2022).

Walker, B W (2020b) Professional Standards and Recognition for UK Personal Tutoring and Advising. *Frontiers in Education*. [online] Available at: https://doi.org/10.3389/feduc.2020.531451 (accessed 14 January 2022).

Yale, A T (2019) The Personal Tutor–Student Relationship: Student Expectations and Experiences of Personal Tutoring in Higher Education. *Journal of Further and Higher Education*, 43(4): 533–44.

Dr Peter Fitch

Peter Fitch is a Lecturer in Teaching at UCL's Arena Centre for Research-based Education. He teaches across the Arena Centre's professional development provision. Peter has responsibility for personal tutoring staff development across UCL. Before joining the Arena Centre, Peter was a Senior Teaching Fellow at Imperial College London. He taught across a range of lecture, practical and fieldwork settings; was personal tutor to undergraduate students, and Senior Postgraduate Tutor for four MSc programmes. Peter has a MEd in University Learning and Teaching. His research interests include taught postgraduate students' learning approaches, digital communities of learning and peer support networks.

Dr Alex Standen

Alex Standen is Associate Professor in Teaching at the Arena Centre for Research-based Education at University College, London (UCL). Alex is responsible for the academic development of early career staff, doctoral supervisors and personal tutors. Her research interests include postgraduate research student development and student–supervisor relationships. She is the co-editor of *Shaping Higher Education with Students: Ways to Connect Research and Teaching* (UCL Press, 2018), in which both students and academics explored how they can work in partnership to advance research-based education.

Abbie King

Abbie King is the Strategic Project Manager (Education & Student Experience) at UCL's Arena Centre for Research-based Education. She works closely with the Arena Centre's leadership team to operationalise its outward-facing activity including: its faculty support work; Arena's input into and support of Quality Assurance and Enhancement processes; and its staff–student partnership activities. Abbie also works to build strong relationships with other UCL central services, ensuring the Arena Centre works effectively and collaboratively on strategic initiatives and projects and that students play an authentic role as our partners in those projects.

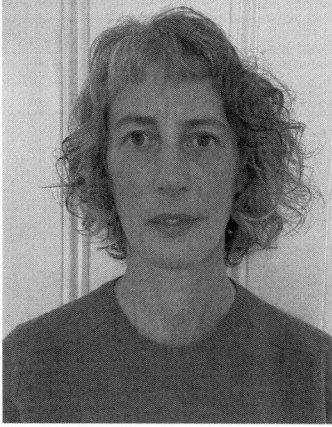

Professor Sam Smidt

Professor Sam Smidt is the Pro-Vice-Provost (Education and Practice Development) and Director of the Arena Centre for Research-based Education at UCL. In the latter role she leads on the strategy related to educational development at UCL and on the support of academic staff in enhancing their learning and teaching practice. A physicist by background, she has many years' experience in online and distance education at the Open University, and has worked on developing and implementing learning and teaching policy. She also has several years' experience working in international education projects, particularly in capacity building projects in Central Asia and in Bangladesh.

Case study 9

'Talking the talk and walking the walk' of personal tutoring: using structured continuing professional development opportunities to inform, develop and empower personal tutors

Rachel George and Eve Rapley

Themes	Page number locations in the companion book
Coaching	15–21, 136–52
Reflective practice	153–67, 170–1
Student involvement and co-creation	61, 107, 116, 167–8
Student peer support	61, 107, 116
Training/Professional development	167–71
Values in personal tutoring and advising	32–9

Introduction

This case study articulates how and why, as experienced personal tutors, we developed two continuing professional development (CPD) workshops for personal tutors at the University of Greenwich, including impacts and recommendations. The first section outlines the context, including student and staff profiles, existing practices, pressures and challenges, and situates these within the wider UK landscape. The next section explores content, underpinning values and delivery modes of the workshops. We articulate our focus on developing and empowering personal tutors through reflective practice. This is followed by initial findings and impact. We close with key learnings and next steps.

Context for the case study

The University of Greenwich is a post-1992 institution of around 19,000 students. With a diverse student and staff body, it has a proud tradition of championing widening participation. Many staff have little prior experience of being either a personal tutor or tutee. Our policy states that all students are allocated a personal tutor, with most programmes using a curricular model (Earwaker, 1992) embedding personal tutoring within a module. Typically, four to six tutorials are offered per year. Tutors are supported by an online Personal Tutor Management System which tracks student engagement.

Personal tutoring literature and our own experience suggest that personal tutoring can suffer from 'patchy' uptake and engagement. This may be attributed to poor understanding of its purpose and attendant value (Yale, 2019) and to inconsistent tutee experiences. While there are many effective tutors in the sector, others may position themselves as fixers and 'saviours' (Clifford, 2019, p 50) or be less engaged or ambivalent about the role. High tutee caseloads can impact on tutor involvement and contribute to tutorials being transactional rather than developmental (McIntosh et al, 2020). This can be further exacerbated when tutors are 'thrown in' to the role (Stuart et al, 2019, p 89) with 'ad hoc' or an absence of training, leaving tutors to learn 'on the job' (Dhillon et al, 2008).

Greenwich is no exception and not immune from these challenges. In the UK higher education landscape where issues of student well-being, finances and satisfaction dominate the discourse, feedback from tutors suggested 'role confusion' (McFarlane, 2016, p 82) and unease about the ever-expanding scope and complexity of the role. Specific concerns included mental health, boundaries, referral, signposting and developing rapport. Frustrations were expressed about navigating policy and guidance. Keen to address these gaps, we devised CPD that spoke directly to our tutors and setting. Mindful of the current higher education context and personal tutoring literature, we aimed to address the concerns of colleagues directly and help them to begin to re-draw the role as one which develops the whole student (Gordon, 1994).

CPD design and content

Our CPD development began in November 2019, with the workshops themselves commencing in March 2020. We drew on the UK Advising and Tutoring association's (UKAT) professional framework (UKAT, 2019b) to inform our design. We felt strongly that a live workshop was necessary to allow for discussion and peer support. We wanted to design CPD that was dialogic, developmental and based on the lived experience of tutoring. We felt this was essential as we believe that personal tutoring CPD cannot be predicated on a model of *telling* colleagues how to do it; rather, it was values-based and set a climate for authentic dialogue

(McFarlane, 2016) using conversation and questions to model a developmental approach (Whitmore, 2017). Participants had opportunities to learn from us and from peers while exploring uncertainties of the role (Darling-Hammond and McLaughlin, 2011).

In addition to the workshops, we created an online hub of resources and guidance and collaborated with our Students' Union to develop personal tutoring 'top tips'. Workshop 1 (two hours) supports staff to be *'Effective personal tutors'*. We chose a topic that would be inclusive, developmental and encourage reflective practice. We invite participants to articulate what effective personal tutoring looks like. Participants draw on experiences of providing (or receiving, for novices) personal tutoring. We prompt reflection not only on what tutors have done before but on why and on how tutees responded.

We then facilitate participants to consider the points raised in relation to principles of effective practice drawn from the literature. Key topics include tutee expectations, communication, boundaries, individual/group tutorials, referrals, signposting, engagement and belonging. The structure is led by examples and shared reflections. We encourage tutors to use asynchronous activities to help make tutorials purposeful and jointly owned with tutees. While acknowledging challenges, we highlight the personal and professional satisfaction experienced when tutees flourish. To encourage impact from the workshop, participants begin action planning for their own personal tutoring context.

Our second workshop (three hours) introduces *'Coaching conversations for personal tutors'*. We encourage tutors to use coaching techniques aimed at empowering their tutees by increasing awareness of their own skills and resources and enabling a more proactive approach to addressing challenges. We support tutors in moving away from viewing personal tutoring as their responsibility to *fix* tutees towards an approach in which tutees are helped to recognise their own potential and maximise agency. We introduce the Goal, Reality, Options, Will (GROW) coaching model (Whitmore, 2017), contextualising this within evidence on benefits of coaching in higher education. Participants take part in practice sets to experience using, responding to, and reflecting on coaching techniques. We support tutors in proposing how they might incorporate this approach in their work with tutees.

With the rapid switch to blended teaching due to Covid-19, we adjusted our content and delivery. We changed from campus-based sessions to delivery via Microsoft Teams using chat and breakout rooms to ensure the sessions remained participant focused. We noted that the online setting facilitated attendance by tutors from the three quite geographically separate campuses. A further benefit was that participating in online CPD helped reduce tutors' anxieties around working with tutees online by building experience and confidence in a low-stakes setting.

In terms of adapting content, while recognising the challenges of the shift online, our starting point was to empower our tutors by encouraging them to recognise their skills from their face-to-face tutoring and think about the many ways in which these would still apply in the blended/online context. There was concern about retention, particularly of first-year tutees. We increased our coverage of topics such as building relationships, supporting engagement and effective communication with personal tutees. We discussed ideas for developing supportive peer groups in the online context, for example, via group tutorials and activities led by near-peers or alumni.

CPD impact and outcomes

To date, in excess of 250 tutors have attended all workshops with initial and ongoing feedback suggesting a positive impact on tutor practice. Participants overwhelmingly report increased confidence and clarity about the role and feel more able to use developmental conversational approaches with a focus on solutions rather than problems (Lochtie et al, 2018). By extension, tutees have benefitted from having tutors who are more confident, informed and empowered.

Improved tutee communications and engagement with more purposeful tutorials have been a key outcome, particularly during Covid-19 and the move online. In the absence of in-person tutorials, tutors report that the investment in building rapport and regular checking in with tutees, to demonstrate interest in them and their well-being, has paid dividends (Starcher, 2011). Improved tutorial attendance and more fruitful dialogue have been reported. In part this has been attributed to using asynchronous activities to give live tutorials more structure and purpose. The investment in creating a tutor group ethos that encourages tutees to recognise shared goals and aspirations, and to mutually support each other (Johnson et al, 2014), has been recognised as beneficial for tutors and tutees. Tutee feedback also suggests the routine check-ins and tutor contact have been vital in the blended/online context (Keeley and Peterson-Ahmad, 2020).

To systematically assess impact, a full evaluation is in progress. We will use questionnaires and focus groups to explore participant experiences of the CPD and its impact on practice. We are currently analysing post-session feedback gathered through Mentimeter and Microsoft Teams chat, and from one-to-one post-session participant de-briefs (n=15) to help inform our September 2021 refresh. We plan to mine programme-level and Students' Union data about student experiences of personal tutoring with a view to ensuring future CPD iterations align with tutee feedback about personal tutoring.

A further significant outcome is a raised profile for personal tutoring at Greenwich. Increased awareness has encouraged an appetite for further CPD, which has been recognised by senior staff. Positive workshop feedback enabled us to secure university funding to obtain UKAT institutional membership (UKAT, 2019a). To help fulfil our longer-term ambitions to have a personal tutoring network of advocates and champions, we are supporting a cohort of over 20 tutors to gain recognition through a UKAT professional development award (UKAT, 2019c).

Future enquiry and scaling

Along with our systematic evaluation of the current workshops, we continue to refine and update them in the light of feedback and sector evidence. We will continue to support tutors to work towards professional recognition and engage with UKAT to ensure our CPD is fit for purpose in an ever-changing and increasingly complex landscape.

Conclusion

From our experience of designing and facilitating structured CPD, it is evident that it has shaped practice and enhanced tutee experiences. It is also apparent that, for impact beyond the immediate reach of individual enthusiastic tutors, CPD needs to be purposeful, structured and planned. Additionally, it requires backing from senior staff to raise its status and emphasise institutional value (Stuart et al, 2019).

Key messages

- Being an effective personal tutor cannot be left to chance; purposeful and planned CPD is essential to support and develop tutors.

- A 'one-stop shop' online resource as a concrete reference point to augment live workshops and consolidate learning is recommended.

- Avoid a deficit model approach and encourage a positive, dialogic position to aid tutee development and enhance their experience.

- Emphasise the significance of the tutor group as a self-supporting peer cohort to function alongside the tutor–tutee relationship.

- Get buy-in from senior management to raise the profile of personal tutoring by positioning the role as strategically significant, and by supporting engagement with external networks and professional recognition organisations such as UKAT (UKAT, 2019c).

- Get buy-in and collaborative involvement from your Students' Union.

Critical reflections

1. If you were designing a personal tutoring CPD session, write down five of the most important attributes (for example, knowledge, skills or attitudes) a personal tutor needs to be 'effective' (based on your own experience).

2. It may be unlikely that teacher training and other courses will prepare you sufficiently for the role. Identify what other informal development opportunities would be beneficial for staff and articulate a rationale for them. Which one of these would you like to personally pursue, develop or implement? Write one small action you could take to initiate it.

3. Do you believe that you can provide an effective personal tutoring service virtually? Are there any additional considerations that need to be planned for both the personal tutoring activity and associated processes? For each point, explain why this is required and important.

References

Clifford, M (2019) Whose Benefit is it Anyway? Dispelling the Deficit Model of Non-Traditional Learners in Higher Education Using Focus Groups. *Educational Futures*, 10(2): 48–65. [online] Available at: https://educationstudies.org.uk/wp-content/uploads/2020/03/BESA-Journal-EF-10-2-3-clifford.pdf (accessed 10 December 2021).

Darling-Hammond, L and McLaughlin, M (2011) Policies that Support Professional Development in the Era of Reform. *Phi Delta Kappan*, 92(6): 81–92.

Dhillon, J K, McGowan, M and Wang, H (2008) How Effective are Institutional and Departmental Systems of Student Support? Insights from an Investigation into the Support Available to Students at One English University. *Research in Post-Compulsory Education*, 13(3): 281–93.

Earwaker, J (1992) *Helping and Supporting Students*. Buckingham: Society for Research into Higher Education and Open University Press.

Gordon, V N (1994) Developmental Advising: The Elusive Ideal. *NACADA Journal*, 14(2): 71–5.

Johnson, D W, Johnson, R T and Smith, K A (2014) Cooperative Learning: Improving University Instruction by Basing Practice on Validated Theory. *Journal on Excellence in College Teaching*, 25(3–4): 85–118.

Keeley, G and Peterson-Ahmad, M (2020) Put Yourself in Their Shoes: How to Check in with Students in an Online Learning Environment. [online] Available at: www.facultyfocus.com/articles/online-education/online-student-engagement/put-yourself-in-their-shoes-how-to-check-in-with-students-in-an-online-learning-environment (accessed 10 December 2021).

Lochtie, D, McIntosh, E, Stork, A and Walker, B W (2018) *Effective Personal Tutoring in Higher Education*. St Albans: Critical Publishing.

McFarlane, K J (2016) Tutoring the Tutors: Supporting Effective Personal Tutoring. *Active Learning in Higher Education*, 17(1):77–89.

McIntosh, E, Steele, G and Grey, D (2020) Academic Tutors/Advisors and Students Working in Partnership: Negotiating and Co-creating in "The Third Space". *Frontiers in Education*, 5: 528683.

Starcher, K (2011) Intentionally Building Rapport with Students. *College Teaching*, 59(4): 162.

Stuart, K, Willocks, K and Browning, R (2019) Questioning Personal Tutoring in Higher Education: an Activity Theoretical Action Research Study. *Educational Action Research*, 29(1): 79–98.

UKAT (UK Advising and Tutoring) (2019a) Benefits of Institutional Membership. [online] Available at: www.ukat.ac.uk/join/institutional-membership (accessed 10 December 2021).

UKAT (UK Advising and Tutoring) (2019b) The UKAT Professional Framework for Advising and Tutoring. [online] Available at: www.ukat.ac.uk/framework (accessed 1 October 2021).

UKAT (UK Advising and Tutoring) (2019c) Professional Recognition. [online] Available at: www.ukat.ac.uk/standards/professional-recognition (accessed 10 December 2021).

Whitmore, J (2017) *Coaching for Performance*. 5th ed. London: Nicholas Brealey Publishing.

Yale, A T (2019) The Personal Tutor–Student Relationship: Student Expectations and Experiences of Personal Tutoring in Higher Education. *Journal of Further and Higher Education*, 43(4): 533–44.

Dr Rachel George

Rachel George previously taught and led courses, and was a personal tutor in psychology at the University of East London. Since 2019, she has worked at the University of Greenwich as Senior Lecturer in HE Learning and Teaching. She has particular interests in personal tutoring, assessment and feedback, and student well-being and is co-editor of the *Compass Journal of Learning and Teaching in HE*. Along with her case study co-author, Dr Eve Rapley, Rachel is currently working towards and mentoring a cohort of Greenwich tutors to gain a UKAT professional recognition award.

Dr Eve Rapley

Eve Rapley began her teaching career in land-based education, specialising in equine science. She has previously taught at the Royal Veterinary College and Imperial College, and holds a part-time bioscience teaching and personal tutoring role at the University of Hertfordshire. During the last ten years, Eve's focus has shifted towards higher education learning and teaching development. Eve is an Associate Professor in HE Learning and Teaching at the University of Greenwich where she leads on personal tutoring. Eve instigated Greenwich becoming a UKAT institutional member, and co-leads the UKAT Professional Recognition Scheme with Dr Rachel George.

Case study 10
Refreshing the academic advising system through co-creation and consensus development

Heather Gray and Sivaram Shanmugam

Themes	Page number locations in the companion book
Boundaries between roles	53–73
Developing a sense of belonging among students	13
Differentiating by subject area	–
Institutional review and implementation	23–5
Personal tutor and advisor forums	–
Postgraduate Certificate in Learning and Teaching in Higher Education	4
Student involvement and co-creation	61, 107, 116, 167–8

Background

Academic advising (AA), often known as personal tutoring in many higher education institutions, has a long tradition in the United Kingdom as it is considered critical in improving students' university experience, satisfaction, retention and success (Montag et al, 2012; McGill et al, 2020). Young-Jones et al (2013) further argue that AA can promote student engagement by serving initially and continuously as an important point of connection, enhancing students' sense of belonging. They also note that academic advisors can interpret institutional expectations and convey them to students in practical terms that illuminate paths to degree completion. Students are more likely to thrive, persist and complete degrees in environments that provide clear and consistent information about institutional expectations and requirements (Tinto, 2007). AA has become even more critical since the onset of the Covid-19 pandemic, as UK survey data identifies that 52 per cent of students report deterioration of their mental health since the pandemic, creating a greater need for AA support (National Union of Students, 2020).

Glasgow Caledonian University (GCU) is one of the largest universities in Scotland with over 1600 staff and 20,000 students across three campuses in Glasgow, London and New York, along with educational partnerships in Oman, Bangladesh and Mauritius. The catalyst for refreshing the AA system at GCU was two-fold; it was: (1) a strategic issue for executive management for enhancing the 'student experience' and (2) a 'big ticket item' in the Students' Association (SA) manifesto. The then President of the SA was a strong proponent of AA, stating that '*AA was vital to the positivity of my experience as a student, building confidence and providing me with a sounding board for my ideas and aspirations*'. Thus, GCU, working alongside the SA, partnered to co-create a refreshed AA system to further enhance students' university experience and sense of belonging.

Methods

We adopted three key principles upon which the process of refreshing GCU's AA system was based: inclusion, consensus development and co-creation with all stakeholders including students, academic and support staff, and senior management. To envision these principles, a cross-university project team was established with academic representation from all schools and the SA President and Vice President for Education. Additionally, for certain stages of the project, doctoral students were employed to assist the project team.

Between October 2017 and May 2018 we undertook the following activities.

1. Co-created a memorable name with accompanying logo for what became the 'Contemporary Academic Advising and Mentoring' (CAAM) Project.

2. Undertook a literature review of the scientific evidence on the role of AA in engendering a sense of belonging and improving student experience and retention.

3. Conducted a scoping exercise of current AA practices across the UK's 167 universities, extracting and summarising key data from university documents and websites.

4. Carried out three consultation workshops with 16 staff and nine students using the Nominal Group Technique consensus development method (Van de Ven and Delbecq, 1972).
   a. During the Nominal Groups participants generated their responses in writing to two specific questions: 'What do you feel are the desired features of an AA system?' and 'What are your expectations of the role of the academic advisor?'

    b.   All generated items were recorded and numbered on flipcharts, after which items were discussed, and similar items amalgamated.

    c.   Participants then ranked their top five items on scoresheets.

    d.   Items with agreement from at least 50 per cent of participants were considered as reaching consensus.

5.   Conducted an electronic survey, using SmartSurvey™, of all GCU's programme leaders (n=65; response rate 60 per cent) to ascertain current AA working practices.

6.   Collated best practice AA case studies from academic staff.

7.   Carried out consultation meetings with key staff from GCU's Student Wellbeing Services and the Student Information Management System.

Project outcomes and impact

Based on the external evidence and the data collected internally, via our survey, consultation meetings and case studies, the key outcome from our project was a co-created, refreshed university AA system. Our Nominal Groups highlighted the key features that students and staff desired from an AA system, the most critical one being 'role clarification'. Therefore, a key project outcome was the co-creation of new role profiles for academic advisors/advisees, programme leaders, programme administrators and heads of departments.

One highlighted element of the academic advisor's role was that it should focus equally on academic and non-academic/pastoral issues, with advisors being a 'first point of contact' and 'listening ear' for students, as well as someone who could 'demystify university processes' and provide profession-specific careers advice.

Another requested feature of the refreshed AA system was a centralised portal of information to support advisors. Therefore, webpages were developed for the role profiles with AA meeting record templates. Additionally, a 'How do I?' website was established for advisors to assist with signposting students.

Timetabled AA sessions were desired by staff and students; however, we recognised that a 'one-size-fits-all' approach was not feasible. Therefore, flexibility was introduced in relation to the timing and format of AA meetings on a programme-by-programme basis.

Quality processes were enhanced to ensure the evaluation of AA through annual programme monitoring processes. Additionally, standardised information on the importance of AA is now included in all module and programme handbooks.

In order to facilitate data capture and evaluation, we campaigned for the inclusion of additional questions in the university's Student Experience Survey to monitor students' uptake of AA and their views on its impact on their studies, awareness of student support services, careers guidance, and support with day-to-day issues. Unfortunately, due to survey fatigue experienced by students, the university decided to stop this survey completely.

In recognition that AA did not feature in the annual Students' Association Teaching Awards, a new category was created entitled 'Super Support' to raise the profile of the academic advisor role.

Factors that contributed to the project's success

The 'buy-in' for the project from the highest levels in the university and the Students' Association was a key success factor, ensuring that the project's progress and recommendations were discussed during strategic committee meetings chaired by the Pro-Vice-Chancellor Learning, Teaching and Student Experience and President of the Students' Association. Furthermore, the fact that our project team had representation from all the schools in the university and included the Students' Association's President and Vice President for Education enabled a two-way flow of information to and from the project team.

Throughout the project our desire was to be as inclusive as possible. Therefore, we felt assured that our student and staff Nominal Groups and survey of all programme leaders enabled sufficient consensus development with appropriate representation from key stakeholders.

Involvement of the university's media team was important, as it promoted the project across the university via on-campus media screens, website, social media and routine communications. Following the launch of the refreshed AA system there was a marketing campaign prompting students to talk to their academic advisor with accompanying videos from staff and students. Furthermore, dissemination occurred at university and school learning and teaching events and a session on 'Demonstrating respect to learners via AA' was incorporated into the Postgraduate Certificate for Learning and Teaching in Higher Education.

Embedding AA into routine quality monitoring processes for academic programmes and keeping it as a standing item on strategic university committee agendas mean that it is regularly reviewed by academic programme teams, quality boards and at executive level.

Recommendations for institutions planning on refreshing their academic advising system

We would recommend that the following aspects are taken into consideration when refreshing any AA system.

- Establish a project team with suitable staff and student stakeholder representation with accountability to a university strategic committee.

- Canvas students and staff for (a) their views on the effectiveness of the current AA system and role of the advisor and (b) suggestions for future enhancement.

- Employ an inclusive, consensus development methodology, such as the Nominal Group Technique, to co-create the new system.

- Assess the AA training needs of staff.

- Review the supporting structures to ensure there are effective mechanisms for quality monitoring and evaluation.

New insights gained

A key insight gained from this project was the fact that although students and staff had similar views on the desirable features of an AA system, their expectations of the role of the academic advisor differed considerably. The top expectations from students, in order of importance, were that advisors: (1) have proper training for the role; (2) provide support to the students on academic and non-academic issues; and (3) provide careers advice. The top role expectations from staff were that advisors: (1) provide advice on academic-related issues; (2) act as a critical friend, providing unbiased advice; (3) are a 'first point of contact' for 'anything', then signpost, accordingly; (4) provide pastoral support; and (5) encourage, motivate and support students through their studies.

These findings highlight the importance of co-creating role profiles for both advisors and advisees. For example, students expected that advisors would provide careers advice, whereas academic staff did not rank this as an important feature. Without a shared understanding of roles, confusion and dissatisfaction can arise from both parties, which could impact negatively upon the uptake and success of AA (McFarlane, 2016; Walker, 2020), running the risk of students feeling unsupported and isolated while experiencing a poorer sense of belonging (Thomas, 2012; Thomas et al, 2017).

Another insight gained was students' negative views of the term AA. They reported that it gave the impression that advisors would only discuss 'academic-related' matters with them and not pastoral issues. The term also caused confusion among international student populations. Therefore, as preferred by students, terms were changed to personal tutoring/tutor/tutee, in common with many other universities.

Key messages

Our key learning points for those refreshing their university's AA system are as follows.

- Secure 'buy-in' from and accountability to a university-wide strategic committee.

- Ensure all relevant student and staff stakeholders from across the organisation are engaged in the re-design and dissemination processes.

- Reflect upon its nomenclature to ensure its acceptability for students and staff.

- Embrace the inclusive philosophies of co-creation and partnership working.

- Consider the use of consensus development methodologies in order to collate and synthesise the views of all key stakeholders and co-create recommendations for change.

Critical reflections

1. If you accept that clarification of the role is important for both students and staff, in your first meetings with your students how would you communicate your view of the role effectively? Also, what are the pros and cons of 'negotiating' the aim and boundaries of the role with students on an individual student-by-student basis?

2. Devise one practical strategy for securing buy-in of current students in helping co-create the personal tutor role and curriculum.

3. What's in a name? Firstly, describe what you feel are the most important activities that a personal tutor performs. Secondly, describe what you feel are the most important student outcomes the role intends to positively influence. Finally, trying to not be influenced by the current term for the role, write down a name(s) which you feel would most effectively communicate the role, its aims and associated activities.

References

McFarlane, K J (2016) Tutoring the Tutors: Supporting Effective Personal tutoring. *Active Learning in Higher Education*, 17(1): 77–89.

McGill, C M, Ali, M, and Barton, D (2020) Skills and Competencies for Effective Academic Advising and Personal Tutoring. *Frontiers in Education*, 5: 135.

Montag, T, Campo, J, Weissman, J, Walmsley, A and Snell, A (2012) In Their Own Words: Best Practices for Advising Millennial Students About Majors. *NACADA Journal*, 32(2): 26–35.

National Union of Students (2020) NUS Student Survey Sends Clear Message to Government – Invest in Mental Health Now. [online] National Union of Students. [online] Available at: www.nus.org.uk/articles/over-half-of-students-mental-health-is-worse-than-before-the-pandemic (accessed 10 October 2021).

Thomas, L (2012) *Building Student Engagement and Belonging in Higher Education at a Time of Change. Final Report from the What Works? Student Retention and Success Programme.* [online] Available at: www.heacademy.ac.uk/sites/default/files/resources/What_works_final_report.pdf (accessed 10 December 2021).

Thomas, L, Hill, M, O'Mahony, J and Yorke, M (2017) *Supporting Student Success: Strategies for Institutional Change. What Works? Student Retention and Success Programme. Final Report.* [online] Available at: www.advance-he.ac.uk/knowledge-hub/supporting-student-success-strategies-institutional-change (accessed 10 October 2021).

Tinto, V (2007) Research and Practice of Student Retention: What Next? *Journal of College Student Retention: Research, Theory, and Practice*, 8: 1–19.

Van de Ven, A H and Delbecq, A L (1972) The Nominal Group as a Research Instrument for Exploratory Health Studies. *American Journal of Public Health*, 62(3): 337–42.

Walker, B W (2020) Tackling the Personal Tutoring Conundrum: A Qualitative Study on the Impact of Developmental Support for Tutors. *Active Learning in Higher Education*. [online] Available at: https://doi.org/10.1177/1469787420926007 (accessed 14 January 2022).

Young-Jones, A D, Burt, T D, Dixon, S and Hawthorne, M J (2013) Academic Advising: Does It Really Impact Student Success? *Quality Assurance in Education: An International Perspective*, 21(1): 7–19.

Dr Heather Gray

Heather Gray is the Head of Physiotherapy and Paramedicine at Glasgow Caledonian University, Chair of the Chartered Society of Physiotherapy's Professional Committee and member of its Equality, Diversity and Inclusion Reference Group. She is currently the lead for the QAA Scotland Collaborative Cluster on building the capacity of academic staff to co-design curricula and co-create teaching and learning environments that are inclusive and promote student mental well-being, particularly for BAME and LGBTQ+ student communities. Prior to this she co-led on three cross-university strategic projects in relation to academic advising, partnership working and student mental well-being.

Dr Sivaram Shanmugam

Sivaram Shanmugam is a senior lecturer, department digital lead, and learning and teaching advisor in the Department of Physiotherapy and Paramedicine. He is also the programme leader of the Doctorate in Physiotherapy (Pre-registration) programme, the first of its kind in Europe. Sivaram co-led the QAA Scotland Collaborative Cluster on building the capacity of academic staff to co-design curricula and co-create teaching and learning environments that are inclusive and promote student mental well-being. Prior to this he co-led on three cross-university strategic projects in relation to academic advising, partnership working and student mental well-being.

Case study 11

Ask PAT: how the introduction and implementation of an e-portfolio approach transformed the nature of student support and development

Celia Greenway

Themes	Page number locations in the companion book
Boundaries between roles	53–73
Institutional review and implementation	23–5
Personal tutor and advisor forums	–
Role types – expert versus generalist; senior and specialised personal tutor and advisor	22–3
Student reflective practice	43, 116

Context

This case study concerns my leadership of the process undertaken for the transformation of the tutorial system by the introduction of an institutional e-portfolio approach at a large Russell Group university with 36,000 students and 7000 staff.

Introduction

One of my main aims for applying for my current strategic leadership role was that I wanted to create policy and implement practice that created confidence in the role of the personal academic tutor (PAT). It has been an overlooked area by the sector and in my institution for over a decade there had been no staff development or review of this key student–staff relationship. Student evaluations (internal and external) of student support indicated there was great variability in the quality of tutoring. The role and approach lacked purpose, poor tutorial attendance indicated that students and staff could not perceive any benefits to the tutorial and there was a tendency to only see your tutor if you had a specific concern. However, the PAT role carries increasing significance in higher education, pivotal to the retention and success of students (Yale, 2019; Walker, 2020). My leadership of the project was underpinned by my academic self, an early years specialist; therefore, to shape the tutorial approach I returned to my doctoral work based on the work of Dahlberg et al (2007). They propose using professional dialogue (meaning making) to create high-quality early years provision and perceive the nursery to be the 'hub' of a community. Embracing their vision for improvement, I wanted to make the tutorial a 'hub' pivotal to the student experience rather than an 'add-on', creating a space for informed dialogue between staff and students.

Project stages

The reasons for choice of reflective model

In order to transform the tutorial approach, I again used my experience in early years and the stance that Loris Malaguzzi embraces in the Reggio Emilia early years approach, regarded as a Global Centre of Excellence for community-based nursery practice. I took the view that everything and everyone is significant in the tutorial process and that by using innovation and creating opportunities for reflection we would enable our students to see '*the future by keeping at hand everything the present gives us today*' (Malaguzzi, 1989, cited in Caligari et al, 2016, p 49). Malaguzzi also proposes that the constant documenting of achievement gives value to the learning journey. Therefore, as part of the transformation of the tutorial system, I decided that using a digital e-portfolio system replicated relevant aspects of this approach. Moreover, as the university's strategic framework (University of Birmingham, 2020) asserts that lifelong learning is the key to ensuring graduates can meet the challenges posed by rapidly changing global, economic, social and digital environments, I used a model of reflection from lifelong learning to generate the tutorial documented dialogue, as shown in Figure 11.1.

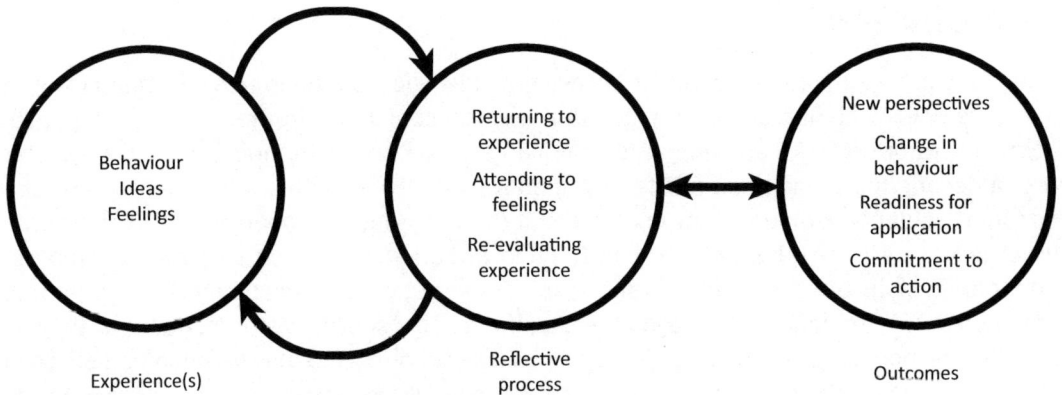

Figure 11.1 *Reflective learning cycle*
(Boud et al, 1985, p 43)

Initial implementation

All students in 2018–19 were introduced to the new e-portfolio as part of our pre-welcome resources. The aim was simple and straightforward. The e-portfolio would support students in preparing for, and getting the most from, their personal academic tutorial meetings. To do this, an online bespoke portfolio was created that invited students to focus on the three areas in the reflective learning cycle when preparing for meetings with their tutor:

* reflection on their learning;

* engagement with assessment;

* preparing for their futures.

This portfolio enabled a joint documentation of their past, present and future. Mirroring social media, students were able to blog and upload photos and recordings. E-portfolios are no longer, in themselves, new technology. Yet, many universities have found it challenging to embed widespread use of these digital tools beyond pockets of innovative practice (Essen, 2017). What distinguishes and makes this project innovative and inspirational is the commitment of the university to ensure that all of its students and staff have access to, and are supported to use, their e-portfolios as part of a lifelong learning approach to personal academic tutoring. All of this was underpinned by my belief that tutorials should optimise student learning and prepare students for their future.

Discussion of initial evaluation findings

Evaluation of the implementation phase in 2019 revealed widespread engagement. Over 80 per cent of first-year students and 60 per cent of all others across undergraduate and postgraduate students' programmes were completing the tutorial reflection activities. To interrogate the quantitative engagement data, focus groups involving staff and students from a representative range of subjects, year groups and role holders were undertaken. The qualitative data indicated that the required pre-tutorial reflective tasks brought a greater focus and structure to the tutorial. The analysis of participant responses showed that by tutors reading the reflections prior to a meeting, more meaningful conversations about personal and academic development were achieved.

Therefore, there was some early success; students were using the e-portfolio to reflect and tutorials were considered more purposeful. The evaluation data indicated that the portfolio process resulted in improved preparation for the tutorial, yet it hadn't increased student confidence in support and development. Thus, it was time, as suggested by Boud et al's model (Figure 11.1), to 'attend to my feelings'. I wanted students to be empowered by their tutorial and to give them agency. Using my theoretical background, in early years terms, I wanted them to be 'strong and capable protagonists', mirroring the approach of Reggio Emilia. Moreover, influenced by the community approach advocated by the early years sector, I wanted the tutorial to be a 'hub' or a 'forum' where shared informed dialogue could be achieved. Malaguzzi (1989, cited in Cagliari et al, 2016) asserts that this informed approach will drive holistic development. A significant amount of work was still needed; the introduction of the e-portfolio had achieved a more purposeful tutorial but it had not achieved an informed shared dialogue.

Post-evaluation actions

Actions in discussion

I realised that reflection, although always espoused as desirable, required both parties in the tutorial process to be more knowledgeable about university services to be effective. The focused dialogue was happening in the tutorials as a result of the e-portfolio approach, yet there were still some 'snagging' issues. Students reported increased satisfaction with the tutorial system; however, referrals to a support service were uninformed. The evaluations suggested that PATs understood their role was to 'signpost' to services but provided advice in a general manner. For example, rather than referring a student to a particular well-being service, well-meaning but often incorrect advice was given, resulting in students having to recount their 'story' several times before finding the most appropriate support. To achieve the original direct aim of students getting the most out of the tutorial, I decided all parties needed to contribute to the 'meaning-making' dialogue and that the e-portfolio needed to be more than a reflective tool. It needed to be a repository, an information 'hub' which empowered students and supported an informed tutorial, as was my desired outcome.

Actions taken for students

The informed tutorial aimed to develop student confidence through the articulation of their support needs and developmental goals. Self-efficacy through the use of e-portfolios is a route well documented by Australian universities (Polly et al, 2015; Yang et al, 2015; Coleman, 2017). Therefore, the next iteration of the e-portfolio used a 'one-stop shop' approach; it now provides information on well-being services, academic support and employability skills. Students now identify how their support needs may be met prior to the tutorial and are encouraged to devise their own action plan. Yet to make this process truly effective for the student, the other participant in the tutorial relationship has to be informed; hence, the last stage of this transformational project focused on the PAT and the leadership of this role. The institution had a number of senior tutors responsible for student support and development; their position mirrored the neglected tutorial system and they were not empowered or informed role holders. They sorted out concerns rather than leading practice. I perceived this role to be pivotal in ensuring the 'hub' approach worked. Arguably a 'hub' needs to be situated in a community, as in the 'Reggio' model. Therefore, I aimed to create a 'Community of Practice' (Lave and Wenger, 2002) with the senior tutors. This theory, like the reflective learning cycle, is also utilised in lifelong learning.

Actions taken for staff

Returning to the cycle, I needed the role holders to be 'committed to action' and to co-construct a revised role descriptor to become leaders in tutoring rather than well-meaning advocates. I established an online learning portal, using the same approach as the e-portfolio, thus everything connected to developing effective tutoring would be in one place. The next step was to encourage 'meaning-making' dialogue by creating a 'Senior Tutor Forum'. The first meeting was well attended, mainly because of their commitment to their students but also due to united concern (and some anger) about the combination of new leadership, uncertainty about the future of their role and the untested e-portfolio approach. The shared forum generated dialogue which informed the role descriptor and the senior tutor team identified their collective professional development needs. This resulted in a series of focused training sessions which are incorporated into the forums. Yet, most significantly, the collective approach has created a strong community of senior tutors and their shared sense of purpose has created a hub of expertise for the PATs and students across the institution.

Key messages

The introduction of the e-portfolio has successfully transformed the nature of student support and development. From the start of 2020, the institution has possessed a purposeful and informed tool for tutorials that is central to the student academic experience, enabling reflection and documenting development. Fullan (1982; Fullan and Stiegelbauer, 1991), writing about educational change, outlines four stages as follows:

1. initiation;
2. implementation;
3. continuation;
4. outcome.

He suggests that to effectively implement change (stage two), the stakeholders, in this study the senior tutors, the PATs, and most importantly the students, need to fully consider a change before committing to the effort of implementation. This perspective is highly pertinent to this case study, and indeed to the higher education sector. The *initiation* was my 'lone' vision, yet the *implementation* has generated *continuation* of shared expertise in the senior tutor team, resulting in an institutional *outcome* that is consistently evolving to suit student needs and creating the intended confidence in the tutoring system.

Critical reflections

1.   If you accept that it is desirable and useful for your students to track their personal development and progress throughout their studies, what aspects do you feel would be most beneficial for them to record?

2.   Do you feel that the leadership of personal tutoring within your department should be separated from the learning and teaching leadership role? Explain why you feel this. What are the advantages and disadvantages of adopting this approach?

3.   Describe key areas which you would want your students to reflect upon when preparing for their one-to-one tutorial. Explain why you feel each is important. Are any of them interrelated and, if so, how?

References

Boud, D, Keogh, R and Walker, D W (1985) *Reflection: Turning Experience into Learning*. London: Kogan Page.

Cagliari, P, Castegnetti, M, Giudici, C, Rinaldi, C, Vecchi, V and Moss, P (2016) *Loris Malaguzzi and the Schools of Reggio Emilia: A Selection of his Writings and Speeches 1945–1993*. London: Routledge.

Coleman, K (2017) *An a/r/t/i/s/t in Wonderland: Exploring Identity Creativity and Digital Portfolios as an a/r/tographer*. PhD thesis, University of Melbourne.

Dahlberg, G, Moss, P and Pence, A (2007) *Beyond Quality in Early Childhood Education and Care: Languages of Evaluation*. 2nd ed. London: Falmer Press.

Essen, E (2017) Do Portfolios Have a Future? *Advances in Health Sciences Education: Theory and Practice*, 1: 221–8.

Fullan, M (1982) *The Meaning of Educational Change*. New York: Teachers College Press.

Fullan, M, and Stiegelbauer, S (1991) *The New Meaning of Educational Change*. 2nd ed. New York: Teachers College Press.

Lave, J and Wenger, E (2002) Legitimate Peripheral Participation in Communities of Practice. *Perspectives on Learning*, 1: 111–26.

Polly, P, Cox, J, Coleman, K, Yang, J L, Jones, N and Thai, T (2015) Creative Teaching, Learning and Assessment in Medical Science: ePortfolios to Support Skills Development in Scientists Beyond Just Knowing Their Own Discipline. In Coleman, K and Flood, A (eds) *Capturing Creativity Through Creative Teaching* (pp 168–82). Champaign, IL: The Learner Series.

University of Birmingham (2020) Our Strategy. [online] Available at: www.birmingham.ac.uk/strategic-framework/overview/birmingham-2026.aspx (accessed 10 December 2021).

Walker, B W (2020) Professional Standards and Recognition for UK Personal Tutoring and Advising. *Frontiers in Education*. [online] Available at: https://doi.org/10.3389/feduc.2020.531451 (accessed 14 January 2022).

Yale, A (2019) The Personal Tutor–Student Relationship: Student Expectations and Experiences of Personal Tutoring in Higher Education. *Journal of Further and Higher Education*, 43(4): 533–44.

Yang, J L, Coleman, K, Das, M and Hawkins, N (2015) Integrated Career Development Learning and E-Portfolios: Improving Student Self-efficacy in Employment Skills in an Undergraduate Science Course. *International Journal of Adult, Community and Professional Learning*, 1: 1–17.

Professor Celia Greenway

Celia Greenway is Director of Student Engagement. In this central university strategic leadership role, she is responsible for the personal academic tutor system, student representation and the enhancement of student engagement. She is a Professor of Education who leads early years education and child development within the university and has contributed to several national reviews of sector policy. Celia has held a number of leadership positions, including the Director of Education and Head of Primary Initial Teacher Education. Her PhD research examined notions of quality within the nursery sector and her subsequent writing has focused upon the initial teacher education sector and approaches to learning within higher education.

Case study 12
Personal tutoring for 'vulnerable' and 'at risk' students: is there value in a differentiated approach?

Sara Hannam and Roger Dalrymple

Themes	Page number locations in the companion book
Data analytics	92–5
Developing a sense of belonging among students	13
Differentiating by individual student needs	108–14
Supporting student populations	75–85
Training/Professional development	167–71
Well-being	13, 23, 55, 179–80

'Vulnerable' and 'at risk' students: the developing context

In recent years, the Office for Students (OfS), the Higher Education Statistics Agency (HESA) and other sector bodies have distinguished an increasing number of 'at risk' student groups, most recently designating international students as within this category during the Covid-19 pandemic (McCluckie, 2014; OfS, 2020a). In parallel, literature such as Lochtie et al's (2018) predecessor text to the current collection have highlighted the specific needs of each group in terms of well-being, success and progression and the junctures of vulnerability each group experiences during the student lifecycle. Yet how far can tutors meaningfully differentiate their tutee cohorts according to these categorisations and would doing so even be helpful to students in terms of enhancing interaction, engagement and support?

Outline of the intervention

Drawing on a shared background in educational development and inclusive practice, we sought to explore how far the increasing number of flags used to identify 'at risk' students might be utilised to support differentiation of the personal tutoring experience. Might they be harnessed for use beyond high-level tracking of student success and progression at programme level? To what extent might demographic information become meaningful *pedagogic* information? In line with Lochtie et al's (2018) recommendations, we envisaged the pedagogic use of student profiles not in terms of subdividing cohorts into sub-groups, or organising meetings with tutees by category, but rather building tutors' awareness of the risks associated with different groups (for example, vulnerability to attrition; vulnerability to poor progression). Such awareness might inform the timing and nature of tutorial encounters and interventions.

To explore this question in our own setting, a post-1992 university in the south-east of England, we engaged with a broad community of personal tutors in two phases. Firstly, we convened an online training session, in collaboration with the institution's educational development team, which combined a short awareness-raising briefing with reflective discussion and a question-and-answer session administered by text chat (over 100 attendees). Secondly, we recruited a smaller pool of participants to two focus groups (n=7 and n=4) to explore these questions in depth using a non-directive approach (Kitzinger and Barbour, 2001) and hypothetical cases. In both the workshop and the focus groups, we supplied a short initial briefing on the current most widely used 'flags' as specified by the OfS and HESA (for example, LGBTQ+, Gypsy Roma Traveller, care experienced), framed by caveats on the importance of ownership of these labels by students themselves through self-identification (OfS, 2020b). Our cases were framed with reference to the literature on employing fictional case studies in educational research (for example, Clough, 2002) and the comparable exemplar cases in the 'at risk monitoring document' supplied by Lochtie et al in the predecessor text (2018, p 84). The hypothetical cases we developed are listed in Table 12.1.

Table 12.1 Hypothetical student cases

Student A	An 18 year-old female (course level 4) care leaver who currently has no fixed address for university holidays.
Student B	A 19 year-old male (course level 5) international student who was unable to get home during the first national 'lockdown' prompted by the Covid-19 pandemic, and who is being supported by the hardship fund.
Student C	A 21 year-old female (course level 6) from a low participation in higher education postcode, from an ethnic minority background who lost a grandparent to Covid-19 in May 2020 and who is being supported to study from home during the pandemic with a university laptop.

Table 12.1 (Cont.)

Student D	An 18 year-old LGBTQ+ male (course level 4) who is registered with the institution's disability services and is a scholarship holder.
Student E	A 23 year-old transgender (course level 5) student ('they') from a traveller background who is making excellent academic progress.

As these examples indicate, we also wanted to ensure that any assumptions regarding the academic progress of 'at risk' students were gently questioned, as we are aware that many students thus categorised may excel at university and that correlations between background characteristics and outcomes are complex and intersectional (Mountford-Zimdars et al, 2015).

The example profiles were shared with the participants who largely confirmed them as reflective of students in their current or past cohorts and who readily supplemented the hypothetical cases with anonymised authentic examples, often relating to LGBTQ+, international and special educational needs and disability students, as well as a number of other categories. Both groups affirmed the value of increased recognition of the complexity of student identities and needs, even if it is not always clear what these identity distinctions mean for personal tutoring practice.

Structured by six prompt questions, the focus groups encouraged participants to reflect on how the categories provide a helpful way into thinking about student needs; whether any of the suggested labels might impact on engagement; whether knowledge of the needs associated with a particular group might enrich or materially change tutee interaction; and whether their tutees have ever identified themselves as, for example, the first in family to go to university. Finally, participants were asked whether personal tutoring should observe a holistic approach or whether differentiation by distinct populations could lead to more personalised and effective student support.

Emerging insights

Three principal insights emerged from the two focus groups, which we report below in order of prevalence and significance in the aggregated data. We utilised a qualitative analysis approach identifying emergent themes (Guest et al, 2013) from notes taken during the two focus groups.

Caution over language

Firstly, there was a pronounced caution in both groups regarding the language used to distinguish 'at risk' student populations. For some colleagues, the notion of labelling (a recurrent term in both groups) was problematic, given the historical precedents for discriminatory or even persecutory use of labels. Others pointed towards the dynamic nature of identity markers and suggested descriptive terms may become unhelpful as they age – shown by the understandable rise in dissatisfaction in the early 2020s with the acronym 'BAME' (Bungwala, 2019; DaCosta et al, 2021). However, most participants recognised the principle that knowing some information about a student was useful in enriching their tutoring practice. References were made to the caution required to ensure that any such information was used sensitively in interactions.

The tutor's role and professional development

Secondly, the role of the tutor was extensively discussed in both focus groups, touching on concerns around the required skill set, training, time needed to form a meaningful relationship, timing of interventions and the crossover with other support available to students. Nomenclature again proved significant given that at our own institution the term employed for the tutor role is 'academic advisor', which can imply a more formal relationship.

Building trust and a safe space

Finally, the dominant view emerging from both groups was that participants would be unlikely to differentiate or tailor their interactions with a tutee based on an awareness of the particular risk factors associated with their ascribed group, at least in the first instance. Instead, tutors emphasised the central role of building trust and offering a safe space so that students could self-identify and disclose in terms of their experience. There were multiple references to conversation as a way of getting to know students so that they could talk in a meaningful way about how their history and identity may or may not be impacting on their time at university.

Conclusion

The sequence of our case study method enabled us to observe first-hand the developing impact of our training workshops on personal tutoring, in terms of consciousness raising and critical engagement with the questions raised. Additionally, having considered all the data deriving from both the training events and focus groups, we have framed the following conclusions for further research, exploration, and for consideration and evaluation in the wider sector.

1. There is value in offering awareness-raising training to personal tutors on the proliferating categories of 'at risk' students and the associated risks for their success and progression. This includes supporting colleagues to recognise the dynamic nature of vulnerability and the role of contingency in students becoming newly vulnerable as circumstances change (as was the case during the onset of the Covid-19 global pandemic).

2. Sharing the lexicon of vulnerable student groups with personal tutors, in a supported context, helps tutors to increase their 'literacy' and engagement around this area and to form richer conceptions of how they might best build rapport and interaction

with students; recognise their distinct, layered and complex needs; and remain attentive to particular areas for support.

3. Sharing hypothetical case studies like those developed in our intervention and those provided in the predecessor text (Lochtie et al, 2018) enables valuable reflection and anticipation of student needs, supporting staff to operationalise this area of their practice.

4. If a 'differentiated' approach to personal tutoring is considered by tutors, this is best understood in terms of building awareness, remaining alert to risk, and offering timely support and intervention rather than any material differences of approach to tutorial conversations and tutor–tutee engagements.

Clearly, these recommendations are best framed in a wider institutional context and our own next steps will involve aligning this work with inclusive curriculum development, particularly centred on induction, transition into and through higher education. We also seek to theorise this work further in the light of principles of Universal Design for Learning (see Bracken and Novak, 2019).

We conclude that it remains more educationally desirable to assume a holistic approach to personal tutoring that is cognisant of discrete student groups but which does not markedly differentiate provision according to pre-established categories so that students retain agency over their identities, and are more likely to build a sense of belonging. Such an approach appears best placed to keep pace with the dynamic nature of vulnerability, not least in the current decade, where public health and social justice agendas have brought renewed and urgent focus to questions of student well-being, identity and belonging.

Critical reflections

1. If you accept that 'knowing your students', building trust and creating a safe space to talk and disclose is the most useful way to understand their immediate support needs, identify three strategies to do this.

2. What techniques do you currently employ to both identify and support students who most need support? Are they effective? How do you know?

3. Does your institution provide personal tutors with data relating to 'at risk' or 'vulnerable' student groups? What are the expectations of how you should use this data? Are these expectations helpful to your personal tutoring practice and the students themselves? Is there any data you feel that would be useful for your practice that you don't already have immediate access to?

References

Bracken, S and Novak, K (2019) *Transforming Higher Education through Universal Design for Learning.* London: Routledge.

Bungwala, Z (2019) Please Don't Call Me BAME or BME! Civil Service Blog. [online] Available at: https://civilservice.blog.gov.uk/2019/07/08/please-dont-call-me-bame-or-bme (accessed 8 October 2021).

Clough, P (2002) *Narratives and Fictions in Educational Research*. Buckingham: Open University Press.

DaCosta, C, Dixon-Smith, S and Singh, G (2021) *Beyond BAME: Rethinking the Politics, Construction, Application, and Efficacy of Ethnic Categorization*. London: Higher Education Research Group.

Guest, G, Namey, E E and Mitchell, M M (2013) *Collecting Qualitative Data: A Field Manual for Applied Research*. London: SAGE.

Kitzinger, J and Barbour, R S (2001) Introduction: The Challenge and Promise of Focus Groups. In Barbour, R S and Kitzinger, J (eds) *Developing Focus Group Research: Politics, Theory and Practice* (pp 1–20). London: SAGE.

Lochtie, D, McIntosh, E, Stork, A and Walker, B W (2018) *Effective Personal Tutoring in Higher Education*. St Albans: Critical Publishing.

McCluckie, B (2014) Identifying Students 'At Risk' of Withdrawal Using ROC Analysis of Attendance Data. *Journal of Further and Higher Education*, 38(4): 523–35.

Mountford-Zimdars, A, Sabri, D, Moore, J, Sanders, J, Jones, S and Higham, L (2015) *Causes of Differences in Student Outcomes*. Bristol: HEFCE.

Office for Students (OfS) (2020a) Supporting Black, Asian and Minority Ethnic Students During the Coronavirus Pandemic. [online] Available at: www.officeforstudents.org.uk/news-blog-and-events/events/supporting-black-asian-and-minority-ethnic-students-during-the-coronavirus-pandemic (accessed 8 October 2021).

Office for Students (OfS) (2020b) English Higher Education 2020: The Office for Students Annual Review. [online] Available at www.officeforstudents.org.uk/annual-review-2020 (accessed 8 October 2021).

Dr Sara Hannam

Sara Hannam is Head of Global Partnerships at Oxford Brookes University, where she leads transnational education strategy and delivery with overseas institutions, including partnerships in China, Sri Lanka, Greece, the Republic of Ireland and others, via Brookes Global. She has a research and teaching background in critical language and sociolinguistics, focusing on inclusive practices in English language teaching, and has extensive experience of teaching and personal tutoring at all levels, in the UK and abroad. Sara has also more recently been involved in chairing a university group set up to identify the needs of vulnerable students during the Covid-19 pandemic.

Dr Roger Dalrymple

Roger Dalrymple is Associate Dean: Student Outcomes at Oxford Brookes University, where he leads on a number of student success, inclusion and progression initiatives. He has a research and teaching background in English and education studies and has extensive experience of personal tutoring systems gained at both pre- and post-1992 universities. He is a member of the British Educational Research Association, Principal Fellow of the Higher Education Academy, and co-editor of Advance HE's case study series on graduate employability.

Case study 13
Supporting Arts and Humanities student development and progression through integrating reflection into personal tutoring

David Lees and Kathryn Woods

Themes	Page number locations in the companion book
Differentiating by subject area	–
Institutional review and implementation	23–5
Pastoral support	21–2, 56
Programme perspective	24, 45–6
Student involvement and co-creation	61, 107, 116, 167–8
Student reflective practice	43, 116

Introduction

Reflective learning involves '*learning how to take perspective on one's own actions and experience... to allow the possibility of learning through experience*' (Amulya, 2004, p 1). Reflection has a strong tradition within education, nursing and professional studies (Rogers, 2001) but is less common within the Arts and Humanities. As the potential of reflection for supporting student progression and holistic development is increasingly understood

(Hughes, 2004), the different ways that reflection can be embedded in personal tutoring across disciplines have begun to be explored (Bassett et al, 2014).

This case study examines how reflective practices were integrated into personal tutoring in the Faculty of Arts at the University of Warwick in 2018–19, and the positive impact this had on students' experiences of personal tutoring and wider learning. It also discusses how reflective learning resources were co-designed with students. The study shows that teaching students how to reflect on their holistic development through personal tutoring helps empower them to manage their academic, personal and career progression at university and beyond.

Personal tutoring in the Faculty of Arts at Warwick

The Faculty of Arts at Warwick employs a pastoral model of personal tutoring (Earwaker, 1992; Thomas and Hixenbaugh, 2006; Lochtie et al, 2018), where students meet their personal tutor once per term. The everyday management of tutoring is largely devolved to departments. Personal tutors have significant autonomy over personal tutoring practice. A review of personal tutoring at Warwick in 2017 revealed that many tutors felt passionate about the role and how it supports students but others felt unsure about its purpose and were awkward about elements of its delivery. Correspondingly, the review showed that students' experiences of personal tutoring were mixed (Warwick University Education Strategy, 2017).

At a strategic level, in 2017, we also noticed that student satisfaction with academic support had begun to decline across the faculty, as indicated by shifting academic support scores in the National Student Survey (NSS) and feedback from student representatives. We believed, from student feedback evidence, that this stemmed from changing student expectations around 'value for money', including in relation to well-being and careers support. Our project exploring the possibilities for embedding reflection in personal tutoring thus aimed to create:

- greater consistency in personal tutoring practice;
- clarity around the purpose of personal tutoring;
- enhanced academic, personal, and careers support for students;
- improved student satisfaction.

Co-creating reflective portfolios

Co-creation with students, defined by Bovill as 'a collaborative approach to the design and creation of learning and teaching experiences' (Bovill, 2013, p 463), is a central element of Warwick's educational philosophy (Warwick Education Strategy, 2018). For this reason, we recruited a small group of personal tutors and students from the School of Modern Languages and Cultures (SMLC) to help us co-create reflective materials for use in personal tutoring. We recruited personal tutors who were interested in developing their practice and students from the Student–Staff Liaison Committee. We asked the students what questions personal tutors should ask when meeting tutees at the start of term.

Using the answers and ideas generated, we subsequently designed a Personal Development and Progress Portfolio. We chose the portfolio model because it enabled continuous dialogue between the tutor and tutee based on their mutual reflections on the latter's strengths, achievements and areas for improvement across the academic year (Hughes, 2004). This portfolio took the form of a series of self-assessment forms which prompted students to reflect upon their learning experiences and their academic, personal, social and employability progression. A system was designed where students would be asked to submit this form electronically, via our attendance system 'Tabula', to their personal tutor before their scheduled termly personal tutor meetings. This would then provide the basis of the conversation between tutor and tutee in the meeting. The number of questions asked of students increased incrementally as they progressed in their degree, culminating in questions around engagement with Student Careers and Skills and their own critical reflection on their academic progress and transferable skills development.

In the SMLC the portfolio was introduced to a trial group of first-year students in term 1 of the 2018–19 academic year. In other departments in the faculty that year, the portfolio was provided as an optional resource that personal tutors could employ in their practice if they wished. In 2019–20, disciplinary tailored versions of the portfolio that was trialled in SMLC were adopted in Classics, English, Theatre, and Film and TV. In the same year, the portfolio was rolled out to all year groups in the School of Modern Languages (circa 360 undergraduate (UG) students). At the time of writing, all departments in the Faculty of Arts at Warwick (circa 2929 UG students) are now delivering some sort of reflective portfolio.

Evaluating success of the reflective portfolios

Evidence suggests that the portfolio was successful in reaching the objectives of our project. In SMLC students gave a 96 per cent satisfaction rating for academic support in the 2018–19 internal Warwick Student Experience Survey (WSES, 2018). This success was echoed across the faculty, especially in departments where the portfolio was widely implemented, with student satisfaction for academic support in the NSS overall rising 8.8 per cent between 2017–18 and 2018–19. Graduate outcomes improved in the same period. In 2020, the Higher Education Statistics Agency (HESA, 2020) ranked SMLC third in the UK on the basis of a recent 'Graduate Outcomes Survey'. Evidence suggests that students especially welcomed the way that the portfolio enables them to track their progression and understand different facets of their educational gain while at university. It also suggests that they value learning the skill of reflection. One student reported that *'the forms help me to keep track of what I've achieved to date on my course. I never really thought about how what we are doing in our modules is actually developing our skills'*. All student feedback highlighted the benefits of a scaffolded approach to the reflective portfolio through which students were supported to reflect critically on their achievements on the course. At the Arts Faculty Education Committee, Heads of Department Forum, and departmental meetings, academic staff have expressed praise for the introduction of the reflective forms and how they give personal tutor meetings structure and promote student engagement.

Conclusion

Implications for learning

Our project identified that Arts and Humanities students can benefit significantly from reflecting on their academic progress and holistic development as part of their university learning. It also identified that by scaffolding – by which we mean the development of a framework in support of – personal tutor meetings we enabled students to learn how to reflect on their experiences of learning and life at university.

We believe that this is just the beginning and that there are many more ways in which reflection can be integrated into personal tutoring. For example, another student who provided feedback on the portfolio noted that one of the downsides of portfolio was that: '*I'd like to be able to have more freedom to write a longer piece like a blog rather than being constrained by the set questions*'. This suggests an appetite for more free-flow text as part of the portfolio. Up until now the portfolios have also been text based but in the future they could be completed in the form of vlogs, audio recordings or graphic images. This could open up exciting avenues for creativity, especially in the Arts and Humanities context. Equally, technology could assist in enabling easier engagement with the portfolio for students and easier data management. It could also perhaps facilitate student engagement with the portfolio before they arrive at university and enable it to be made exportable to students when they graduate, and to potential employers.

In summary, our project demonstrated that there is a firm place for reflection in personal tutoring. It showed that engaging in reflection and learning reflective skills can have a range of benefits for students, and that there are a multitude of ways that reflection in personal tutoring can be developed to boost student experience but also equip students to be more self-aware. The methods our project employed – co-creating reflective resources with students and using reflective forms to facilitate and structure student reflection through personal tutoring – are easily transferred to other disciplines as well as personal tutor systems in different university contexts and, as the case study has shown, enable materials to be tailored to the needs of different study populations and disciplines.

Critical reflections

1. Identify and rank in order (one being the most useful) three aspects of personal tutoring practice and management within your workplace context, which would most benefit from students working closely in partnership with staff to improve the student experience (in other words, co-creation). For each aspect, describe how you feel this would improve the students' experience.

2. If you accept that developing students' ability to reflect upon their learning is beneficial to their performance, evaluate what role personal tutoring plays in developing this at your institution. How might this be developed further?

3. Explain three practical strategies to encourage and help students to prepare for a one-to-one meeting or group tutorial session.

References

Amulya, J (2004) What is Reflective Practice? [online] Available at: www.itslifejimbutnotasweknowit. org.uk/files/whatisreflectivepractice.pdf (accessed 10 December 2021).

Bassett, J, Gallagher, E and Price, L (2014) Personal Tutors' Responses to a Structured System of Personal Development Planning: A Focus on 'Feedback'. *Journal for Education in the Built Environment*, 9(1): 20–34.

Bovill, C (2013) Students and Staff Co-Creating Curricula: An Example of Good Practice in Higher Education? In Dunne, E and Owen, D (eds) *The Student Engagement Handbook: Practice in Higher Education* (pp 461–76). Bingley: Emerald.

Earwaker, J (1992) *Helping and Supporting Students: Rethinking the Issues*. Buckingham: Society for Research into Higher Education and Open University Press.

Higher Education Statistics Agency (HESA) (2020) Graduate Outcomes Survey. [online] Available at: www.hesa.ac.uk/news/18-06-2020/sb257-higher-education-graduate-outcomes-statistics (accessed 10 December 2021).

Hughes, S (2004) The Mentoring Role of Personal Tutoring in the 'Fitness for Practice' Curriculum: An All Wales Approach. *Nurse Education in Practice*, 4(4): 271–8.

Lochtie, D, McIntosh, E, Stork, A and Walker, B W (2018) *Effective Personal Tutoring in Higher Education*. St Albans: Critical Publishing.

Office for Students (2018) National Student Survey (NSS) 2018. [online] Available at: www.office forstudents.org.uk/advice-and-guidance/student-information-and-data/national-student-survey-nss/nss-2018-results (accessed 10 December 2021).

Office for Students (2019) National Student Survey (NSS) 2019. [online] Available at: www.office forstudents.org.uk/advice-and-guidance/student-information-and-data/national-student-survey-nss/nss-2019-results (accessed 10 December 2021).

Office for Students (2020) National Student Survey (NSS) 2020. [online] Available at: www.office forstudents.org.uk/advice-and-guidance/student-information-and-data/national-student-survey-nss (accessed 10 December 2021).

Rogers, R (2001) Reflection in Higher Education: A Concept Analysis. *Innovative Higher Education*, 26(1): 37–57.

Thomas, L and Hixenbaugh, P (2006) *Personal Tutoring in Higher Education*. Stoke-on-Trent: Trentham Books.

Warwick University Education Strategy (2017) Warwick Personal Tutoring Review. [online] Available at: https://warwick.ac.uk/about/strategy/education/detail/case-studies/perstutoring (accessed 10 December 2021).

Warwick University Education Strategy (2018) [online] Available at: https://warwick.ac.uk/about/strategy/education/detail/education_strategy.pdf (accessed 10 December 2021).

Dr David Lees

David Lees is Associate Professor of French and Deputy Dean of Students at the University of Warwick. He teaches and researches aspects of French politics, history and culture. In addition to his principal role as Director of UG Studies in the School of Modern Languages and Cultures, David is also currently the Faculty Senior Tutor for Social Sciences. David is a regular contributor to national and international media on aspects of French and European culture, politics and history.

Dr Kathryn Woods

Kathryn Woods is Dean of Students at Goldsmiths, University of London. She is responsible for leadership and enhancement of the student academic experience, with a particular focus on personal tutoring. From 2017 to 2020, Kathryn was Director of Student Experience for the Arts Faculty at the University of Warwick, during which time she was also Director of the Digital Arts Lab. Kathryn has a PhD in History from the University of Edinburgh. She has published widely on identity, community and the body in eighteenth-century Britain, as well as personal tutoring and the student academic experience.

Case study 14

A 'whole of institution' approach: what does a culture of advising and tutoring really involve?

Emily McIntosh, Deeba Gallacher and Alex Chapman

Themes	Page number locations in the companion book
Boundaries between roles	53–73
Data analytics	92–5
Developing a sense of belonging among students	13
Embedded into teaching	22
Group personal tutoring and advising	108–17
Personal tutoring and advising curriculum	122–1
Role definition	12–14
Student engagement	44, 56, 57, 58–60, 66–7
Supporting student populations	75–85
Transition	105–8
Well-being	13, 23, 55, 179–80
Whole-institution approach	24

Introduction

In this case study we reflect on the role of advising and tutoring (hereafter advising) in pedagogical practice, how it aligns with institutional strategies, structures and models and why it informs a holistic 'whole of institution, whole of student' (Kift and Nelson, 2005) culture of student success. We showcase an integrated model of advising at Middlesex University (MDX), London, reflecting on the role of advisors in realising this cultural shift. We draw on components of advising practice, such as advising for students in transition, the design of a tutorial curriculum, and systems to support signposting and referral. We explore the impact of advising on student learning and assessing outcomes for vulnerable student groups. Finally, we reflect on the benefits of advising as a key pedagogical practice, a relational form of pedagogy (Bovill, 2020) and a critical component of '*relationship-rich education*' (Felten and Lambert, 2020). We consider the impact of advising masterclasses and apply this to blended modalities, especially in the wake of the Covid-19 pandemic, and reflect on scaling advising infrastructure. Throughout we draw upon evidence and literature to support our insights, in particular Lochtie et al's (2018) *Effective Personal Tutoring in Higher Education*.

Overview of Middlesex University, London

Middlesex student profile

Middlesex is a post-1992 widening participation university based in Hendon, North London. We have a diverse student profile, with around 24,000 students studying in London, Dubai and Mauritius. In London, 68 per cent of our students are home domiciled, 16 per cent from the EU and 16 per cent are international. Eighty-seven per cent of our students fall into at least one widening participation category. One-third (32 per cent) are first-generation students from low-income households (Index of Mass Deprivation (IMD) quintiles one and two). Forty-five per cent of our students are first-generation students. Nine per cent of our students have a disability. Three in ten of our students (28 per cent) are mature (21 and above). Seventy-one per cent are from an ethnic minority background, compared to a national average of 16 per cent. We have ten per cent more students from the most disadvantaged neighbourhoods compared to the national population. Middlesex has the highest percentage of students eligible for free school meals (FSM) of any UK higher education institution (52 per cent). Finally, a third of our students enter university with BTEC qualifications, and those with BTECs (specialist work-related qualifications) are twice as likely to be of black ethnicity.

Advising and strategy: alignment with pedagogic practice

The increasing significance of advising coincides with unprecedented change, with UK universities navigating volatile trends in government policymaking and the impact of the Covid-19 pandemic. Educational disadvantage persists for several student groups, such as those from (1) Black, Asian and Ethnic Minority backgrounds, (2) students with mental health issues and disabilities and (3) those from low-income households (Mountford-Zimdars et al, 2015). The pandemic has likely exacerbated these disparities. The emergency pivot online in Spring 2020 and the implementation of blended models of learning has underscored the importance of an approach built around belonging, and systems which foster relationships and dialogue. Advising stands at the forefront of student-centred strategy, where several infrastructural components are implemented and embedded. Advising works especially well in a flipped and blended approach, supported by digital infrastructure and technology, and is fundamental to achieving ambitions around the agenda for equality, diversity and inclusion, and decolonisation of the curriculum (McIntosh et al, 2020). Advising systems must be supported and championed at every level of the organisation and receive prominence in institutional education strategies.

The Student Success Tutoring project @ MDX

In 2019 we re-configured our existing advising approach, formalised by the Student Success Tutoring (SST) project. The Middlesex model has several evidence-based components, providing an organisational approach to academic support. In September 2020, ten academic programmes began piloting our new approach. These programmes have worked with the project team since November 2019 in an initial onboarding phase (November 2019 to September 2020). The advising infrastructure at Middlesex is designed to improve student outcomes; the components are as follows.

- Piloting an integrated model of advising – in 1992, Earwaker outlined the professional, curricular and pastoral models of advising, and these have been reconsidered in recent literature (Lochtie et al, 2018, pp 21–3 and 35–6). The integrated model of advising (McIntosh, 2018) develops these critical elements into one multi-agency, collaborative model of advising designed to improve structural and systemic barriers. Our definition of advising describes 'personal tutoring' as something provided by the institution, where various stakeholders perform different advising functions within that space, working collaboratively.

- Developing a tutorial curriculum – the SST project is piloting a tutorial curriculum which considers advising interactions embedded within the curriculum and aligned with the student lifecycle. The tutorial curriculum is designed to promote engagement with advising as a core feature of the learning journey, considering the ultimate balance between group and one-to-one student/tutor interactions. In the first phase, six advising interactions are being piloted.

- Timetabled – to establish advising as core pedagogic practice, tutorials are timetabled to encourage engagement. A balance of timetabled, synchronous group tutorials, based on the tutorial curriculum, encourages a sense of belonging, connectedness and cohort identity. This supports and facilitates independent, one-to-one asynchronous activity.

- Flipped approaches to advising – getting the balance right between synchronous and asynchronous activity is important. In line with our technology enhanced learning (TEL) framework, advising is flipped so that *before* tutorials students are encouraged to interact with content in the virtual learning environment (VLE), so that engagement *during* (synchronous, group) and *after* (asynchronous, group and one-to-one) is more fluid.

- Integration of learning technologies – the model is supported by learning technologies, emphasised in Chapter 4 of *Effective Personal Tutoring in Higher Education*. Beyond the VLE (Moodle), we have introduced the 'StREAM' Dashboard to support learning and engagement analytics. We are using the 'Fika' app (Fika, nd) to support curricular well-being conversations. The 'StREAM' Dashboard provides dynamic information on learning analytics for personal tutors to use to inform their conversations. The 'Fika' app (Fika, nd) is designed to support conversations around mental health and well-being and has a number of structured activities for tutors and students to use.

- Streamlining signposting and referral – we have streamlined signposting and referral to central and specialist support teams. This supports academic colleagues to signpost students to support outside of their immediate area of expertise, as emphasised in Chapter 3 of *Effective Personal Tutoring in Higher Education*.

- Masterclasses – advising masterclasses, focused training sessions with experts, have been provided, where different stakeholders explore the components of the revised model. Initial masterclasses focusing on a rationale for the approach were followed by more detailed masterclasses looking at applying the components in practice. Many of the masterclasses expand the concepts outlined in the literature (Lochtie et al, 2018).

- Follow-up meetings – scheduled follow-ups with each programme team discussed the application of the model. As a continuous improvement exercise, these were designed to support colleagues to develop their practice and identify areas of improvement.

Evaluation and impact

We developed an Evaluation and Impact Framework to measure three types of outcome longitudinally: (a) student outcomes; (b) staff outcomes and (c) institutional outcomes. Our framework ensures that we measure these both quantitatively and qualitatively, capturing progress. A first-stage evaluation questionnaire was circulated to all programme leads who participated in the pilot approach. Twenty-one responses to the anonymous questionnaire were received. The evaluation revealed that advisors have adopted online approaches to advising in response to the pandemic. Online tutoring is popular, with Zoom adopted as the platform of choice. Online advising has provided flexibility and is more accessible for staff and students, making it easier to meet students without the need to book rooms. Respondents observed that the integrated model has offered a clear structure and purpose to advising meetings. The opportunity to have discussions in small groups was welcomed, and this helped build relationships between students. Over 75 per cent of respondents indicate that they have held one-to-one meetings with students in addition to group tutorials. Student attendance and engagement has improved, and respondents believed engagement in personal tutor meetings was comparable with other online teaching sessions. Tutor self-reported data indicates that approximately 56 per cent of students engaged regularly with personal tutorial sessions. Almost all respondents have used 'Fika' (Fika, nd) with their students during the last year. The majority of respondents indicated that their programme has adopted group tutorials and over 70 per cent indicated that structured interactions have been implemented, according to the tutorial curriculum. *Wellbeing, Pressing Pause* and *Settling In* were the most commonly implemented interactions.

Student outcomes

We anticipate several longitudinal student outcomes as part of this project, as follows.

* Greater facilitation of learner autonomy and group cohesion.
* Managing expectations and preparedness for study.
* Focusing on the learning journey – anticipating transitions and adjustment.
* Better outcomes – first-time pass, continuation and achievement.
* Improving the visibility of well-being within the curriculum.
* Higher reported levels of student self-efficacy and confidence.
* Higher reported levels of student satisfaction.
* Greater participation in co- and extracurricular activities.

Staff and institutional outcomes

We also anticipate several longitudinal staff and institutional outcomes as part of this project, as follows.

* Greater understanding of, and participation in, advising as a core pedagogical practice.
* Greater engagement with learning from staff and students.
* Greater level of emerging best practice in advising, with advising learning outcomes.
* Higher reported levels of colleague satisfaction.
* Higher levels of progression (year on year).
* Reduction in awarding and attainment gaps for vulnerable student groups.
* Student voice, co-design and partnership established as a key part of a relational approach.
* Early intervention and transitional support, which is agile and flexible, established as a core curricular philosophy.

Conclusion

Our focus on an infrastructural approach to advising, implementing the key components outlined above, is intended to transform the Middlesex learning journey. We believe that there are several implications for sector-wide advising practice. We have learnt that taking an affiliative, dialogic approach to advising, where we focus on an integrated model, in conversation with colleagues and students, has engaged colleagues and supported them to apply the components in their own discipline. Online tutoring has been a success and, longitudinally, we hope that this continues to be reflected in our student, staff and institutional outcomes. Structured curricular group interactions are also preferred by advisors, as are opportunities to bring in appropriate technologies like 'Fika' (Fika, nd), and this appears to have had a positive impact on student engagement. Future research will help us to better understand the impact of this model on reaching our most vulnerable students, helping to focus and scale the integration of best practice.

Critical reflections

1. Can a whole-institution approach to personal tutoring and advising be considered in isolation from the same for learning and teaching? Are they interrelated at your institution? If yes, how? If no, would it help if they were and why?

2. As a member of staff involved in personal tutoring:

   a. which of the student outcomes do you achieve well and why? Describe one small action that could be taken to share this good practice.

   b. which of the student outcomes would you like to 'do better' on and why? Describe one small action that could be taken to improve.

   c. which of the institutional outcomes do you feel most invested in improving and why? Describe one small action you could take to influence this for either your students, course, department or faculty.

3. The case study by Brown and Thomas (Case study 5) explains that individuals define what is meant by 'student success'. With this in mind, rank the student outcomes in order of which criteria is most important to your definition of student success, number one being the most important and so on. Are there any additions or changes you would make to the list and why?

References

Bovill, C (2020) *Co-Creating Learning and Teaching: Towards Relational Pedagogy in Higher Education*. St Albans: Critical Publishing.

Earwaker, J (1992) *Helping and Supporting Students: Rethinking the Issues*. Buckingham: Society for Research into Higher Education and Open University Press.

Felten, P and Lambert, L (2020) *Relationship-Rich Education*. Baltimore, MD: Johns Hopkins University Press.

Fika (nd) Mental Fitness. [online] Available at: www.fika.community (accessed 14 January 2022).

Kift, S and Nelson, K (2005) *Beyond Curriculum Reform: Embedding the Transition Experience*. Hammondville, Australia: Higher Education Research & Development Society of Australasia (HERDSA) Conference Proceedings.

Lochtie, D, McIntosh, E, Stork, A and Walker, B W (2018) *Effective Personal Tutoring in Higher Education*. St Albans: Critical Publishing.

McIntosh, E (2018) The 4 Step Tutorial Pathway – A Model of Early Intervention & Transitional Support (EI) to Facilitate Resilience and Partnership Working in Personal Tutoring. Paper presented at the UK Advising and Tutoring (UKAT) Conference, 27 March 2018, Derby.

McIntosh, E, Steele, G and Grey, D (2020) Academic Tutors/Advisors and Students Working in Partnership: Negotiating and Co-creating in 'The Third Space'. *Frontiers in Education*, 5: 528683.

Mountford-Zimdars, A, Sabri, D, Moore, J, Sanders, J, Jones, S and Higham, L (2015) *Causes of Differences in Student Outcomes*. Bristol: HEFCE.

Dr Emily McIntosh

Emily McIntosh joined Middlesex University, London in 2019 as Director of Learning, Teaching and Student Experience with responsibility for leading several strategic, cross-institutional initiatives including academic development, technology-enhanced learning, student engagement and transition, inclusion in the curriculum, academic advising and tutoring, and learning analytics. She is a Principal Fellow of the Higher Education Academy (PFHEA), and National Teaching Fellow (2021). From 2016–21 Emily was Vice-Chair (Research), Trustee and Board Member of UKAT (UK Advising and Tutoring), the cross-sector organisation championing advising and tutoring in higher education. Emily's research focuses on the impact of advising and tutoring, peer learning and learning analytics.

Dr Deeba Gallacher

Deeba Gallacher is Head of Academic Practice Enhancement at Middlesex University with 20 years of experience in educational development. Spending a decade as a research fellow, Deeba adopts an evidence-based approach, foregrounding institutional research to implement large-scale cultural change. Her interests and work focus on the student experience and transitions, equality, diversity and inclusion within the curriculum, and supporting colleagues in their professional development and recognition of their practice through the UK Professional Standards Framework, National Teaching Fellowship and Collaborative Award for Teaching Excellence. Following a MSc in Research Methods and a PGCHE, Deeba received her EdD in 2012, focusing on institutional culture and student retention and progression. She is a Senior Fellow of the Higher Education Academy.

Alex Chapman

Alex Chapman joined Middlesex University in June 2007, having worked previously at the Learning Technology Section, Edinburgh University and the Centre for Academic Practice, Queen Margaret University. Alex has over 15 years' experience of supporting and leading on educational technology in higher education and has led on a number of key university initiatives such as the implementation of Middlesex's Technology Enhanced Learning Threshold Standards. He is currently working on the university's Student Success and Tutoring project, aligning the approach to personal tutoring and student engagement data and analytics. Alex has completed his PGCHE and is a Fellow of the Higher Education Academy.

Case study 15

Levelling up: from reactive to proactive – shifting the narrative of academic tutoring from problems to solutions

Amanda Millmore, Jo Cordy, Jess Johnson, Cindy Isherwood, Ed White, Lillie-Mae Firmin, Fifi Bangham and Orla Kennedy

Themes	Page number locations in the companion book
Boundaries between roles	53–73
Institutional review and implementation	23–5
Role types – expert versus generalist; senior and specialised personal tutor and advisor	22–3
Student engagement	44, 56, 57, 58-60, 66–7
Supplementary support for personal tutoring and advising	22
Whole-institution approach	24

Introduction

How do you transform personal tutoring from a reactive to proactive model? At the University of Reading, an institution-wide project undertaken since 2016 has successfully remedied many of the failings of our former deficit model of personal tutoring to become a model of genuine partnership, engagement and development, which works across the institution and provides a more consistent student experience.

Redesigning the tutor system

The University of Reading is home to more than 19,000 students from over 150 countries (University of Reading, nd). Previously, each student had a personal tutor (supported at departmental level by a senior tutor) but there was a lack of consistency in students' experience, tutors felt overburdened by pastoral responsibilities and senior tutors lacked any central support. Having identified significant dissatisfaction with our personal tutoring approach, through staff and student surveys, we established a project to improve the system.

The University of Reading acknowledges the crucial role that tutoring plays in supporting the success of all students (Stenton, 2017). We remained committed to retaining one-to-one tutoring with dedicated academic staff but needed to find ways to improve the experience for staff and students.

Avoiding the pitfalls of a top-down institutionally imposed revamp, critical to our success was extensive consultation over many months to identify the issues, engaging critical stakeholders at every stage (Hodges, 2016).

We formed a steering group, with cross-stakeholder membership, including student representatives, academic and support staff, institutional leadership and project management support; all the right people 'on the bus' (and reflected in this case study's authorship). The steering group oversaw the project design, was integral to the launch of the new system and monitored its impact and transformation into 'business as usual'. In this way we ensured not only 'top-down' support, but 'bottom up' 'buy in' to the project. This high level of consultation was unusual for university projects but is now viewed as an example of good practice at institutional level (University of Reading, 2021).

As part of the project re-design, we identified six core principles which would underpin the Academic Tutor System (ATS) to ensure that student success is at its heart and to guide the restructuring process. These were as follows:

- equitable access for all taught students;
- communication of benefits, roles and responsibilities;
- referral to specialist support for pastoral care;
- proactive relationships and shared responsibilities;
- promotion of student engagement and belonging;
- support for academic, personal and professional development.

Critically, we reframed the tutor–tutee relationship from hierarchical roles into a partnership supporting students' academic, personal and professional development.

The steering group met regularly, with key stakeholders as workstream leads responsible for driving forward change. The workstreams focused upon staff and student engagement, student services, institutional change and project management. This devolution of responsibility enabled frequent stakeholder consultation and regular monitoring by the steering group, ensuring the project remained on track within its timetable.

The new Academic Tutor System

We launched the newly evolved system in Autumn 2018, with new roles for tutors and improved leadership within schools. Crucially, a new welfare team was created as part of student services, offering pastoral support to students (and staff) for many issues affecting our students; this has been a vital layer of support during the Covid-19 pandemic.

The key features of the new system are as follows.

- Focus on students' academic, personal and professional development.
- Partnership with professional support services to support students with personal challenges that may impact their studies.
- School-level leadership provided by School Directors of Academic Tutoring.
- Central support provided for students and staff.

New focus: academic, personal and professional development

We have retained the one-to-one tutor/tutee relationship in the university, but the reframing and renaming of this relationship has been fundamental to its success. The personal tutor system often left academic staff overburdened and feeling unqualified to meet students' support needs. The new ATS was designed to allow academic staff to play to their strengths and focus upon supporting tutees academically and professionally, with an eye on students' personal development. Communication was key to ensuring that tutors understand that while approachability and empathy are key to the role (Lochtie et al, 2018), ongoing support for students' personal difficulties is outside their remit. We equipped our tutors with a clear signposting framework to relevant professionals within the university. Our UK Engagement Survey (UKES) (Advance HE, 2021) results show an 11.3 per cent increase in satisfaction with the tutor relationship between 2018 and 2020.

Similarly, our UKES results show a 14.9 per cent increase in satisfaction with signposting from 2018 to 2020 and tutors now feel more confident in doing this, with greater awareness of available support services. Acknowledging the shift in their role enables academic tutors to build professional partnerships with their tutees, establishing relationships which encourage proactive rather than reactive tutoring.

Improved partnerships: schools and student services

The introduction of the new student welfare team (a manager and six student welfare officers, allied to specific schools) as part of the student services' portfolio has been critical to the success of the ATS.

The remit of the welfare team is to support students with personal issues affecting their studies, such as bullying, homesickness and family difficulties. They operate a holistic 'team around the student' approach to support (Limbrick, 2001). The welfare team has become embedded within our support services and exists as a referral option for staff within schools and as a drop-in service for students, distinct from our therapeutic counselling and well-being team. Good links between schools and their designated welfare officers have led to effective interventions on both sides. In 2018–19 the team engaged with 899 students, increasing to 1042 in 2019–20, with over 50 per cent of these self-referring via the drop-in service. Student satisfaction indicated that 89 per cent would recommend the welfare team to a friend.

A support services' flowchart document was created and welcomed by tutors as it allows them to clearly identify support services and signpost students appropriately.

Leadership: the School Directors of Academic Tutoring (SDATs)

As part of the reframing of the academic tutor role, leadership of the system within schools has been improved. The earlier system's senior tutors were often the poor relations of other Teaching and Learning leadership positions, whereas SDATs have been encouraged to think strategically in overseeing student engagement, success and retention (University of Reading, 2020).

This leadership role is recognised contractually with a minimum time allocation and a formal selection process, bringing parity with other school leaders. Crucially, SDATs are routinely invited to school and institutional committees, bringing their strategic, student-focused approach to discussions. Greater recognition is long overdue but has enhanced the standing and importance of the ATS.

Central support

As an institutional project there has been good communication directly with staff and students about the changes, with provision of ongoing support resources to maximise the tutor–tutee relationship. We have created online toolkits for tutors and tutees, with information in the staff toolkit reflected in the student equivalent so that both groups receive the same mirrored messages. Use of these online resources has increased year on year, with data analytics showing that engagement with the online student resources increased by 13 per cent from 2018–19 to 2019–20.

Information can be cascaded quickly from institutional level via the SDATs through their effective community of practice, and their concerns and suggestions for improvement can be transmitted swiftly back to the university leadership. Improved communication has been a key driver for success, with notable benefits being student postcards promoting the ATS, student video guides about getting the most from the tutor–tutee relationship, staff paper guides to the ATS and signposting flowchart (which adorns many noticeboards) and continuing professional development (CPD) sessions for staff. This two-way flow of dynamic communication has been central to appropriately supporting students during Covid-19.

Impact and evaluation

Three years on, the ATS is now our usual practice and successful key impacts have been realised as follows.

- Students have given increased ratings for academic support in both the UKES and the National Student Survey (NSS) since 2018 (OfS, 2021).

- Tutors have seen improved student engagement since the launch of the ATS. A survey of tutors showed that 57.4 per cent of respondents had met with more than two-thirds of their tutees in 2019–20, an increase of five percentage points since 2018–19.

- School Directors of Academic Tutoring are empowered to lead change to support their students and tutors, particularly during the Covid-19 pandemic where their involvement in high-level decision making has helped to ensure a student-focused approach.

- Schools and professional student support services have experienced improved connectivity with vibrant communities of practice established to share best practice and implement change and continuous improvement.

Key messages

Culture change in a large organisation takes careful planning and persistence (Hodges, 2016), but we have seen excellent progress and success with our ATS project. Key themes from our experience have become apparent as follows.

Communication

Change management and effective communication is required, not just at the consultation stage, but throughout the project (Butt et al, 2016). The creation of mirrored resources for tutors and students have been vital to ensure consistency across the university, as has the evolution of those resources to meet tutor/tutee needs. For example, staff surveys indicated a number of persisting myths about the ATS, and myth-busting formed part of CPD provision.

'Top-down'/'bottom up' support

Project sponsorship by senior management and alignment to strategic priorities are critical to success, as is engagement and acceptance from tutors and student engagement. Equally, without the institutional funding for the new welfare team, it would have been difficult to truly shift from pastoral/reactive tutoring to proactive academic tutoring. The welfare team is securely embedded within the institution and their support role is highly praised by academics and students alike.

Play to your strengths

The new ATS acknowledges the strengths of academics in advising about academic, personal and professional development and this new system enables tutors to do what they do best. Raising the profile and visibility of professional support services across the university has ensured that students and staff are happier with their tutor relationship and everyone is more effectively supported.

Critical reflections

1. Analyse why it is important for both personal tutors and students to have clarity over how far a tutor can support with a student's 'personal difficulties'.

2. To what extent is effective boundary setting between personal tutors and students emphasised and supported at your institution? Write small actions you could take to help move this forward.

3. While a 'bottom-up' rather than 'top-down' approach to organisational change has clear benefits, identify two potential issues with implementing this. How might you overcome them?

References

Advance HE (2021) *UK Engagement Survey (UKES)*. [online] Available at: www.advance-he.ac.uk/reports-publications-and-resources/student-surveys/uk-engagement-survey-ukes#reports (accessed 10 December 2021).

Butt, A, Naaranoja, M and Savolainen, J (2016) Project Change Stakeholder Communication. *International Journal of Project Management*, 34(8): 1579–95.

Hodges, J (2016) *Managing and Leading People Through Organizational Change*. London: Kogan Page Limited.

Limbrick, P (2001) *The Team Around the Child: Multiagency Service Co-ordination for Children with Complex Needs and Their Families*. UK: Interconnections.

Lochtie, D, McIntosh, E, Stork, A, and Walker, B W (2018) *Effective Personal Tutoring in Higher Education*. St Albans: Critical Publishing.

Office for Students (OfS) (2021) National Student Survey (NSS) [online] Available at: www.officeforstudents.org.uk/advice-and-guidance/student-information-and-data/national-student-survey-nss/get-the-nss-data/#datafiles (accessed 10 December 2021).

Stenton, A (2017) Why Personal Tutoring is Essential for Student Success. [online] Available at: www.heacademy.ac.uk/blog/why-personal-tutoring-essential-student-success (accessed 10 December 2021).

University of Reading (2020) *SDAT Role Description*. [online] Available at: https://sites.reading.ac.uk/academictutors/wp-content/uploads/sites/38/2020/11/ATSpolicy_Appendix4_roleandresponsibilitiesSDATs.pdf (accessed 10 December 2021).

University of Reading (2021) Winners Announced for University Collaborative Awards for Teaching and Learning 2021 – University of Reading. [online] Available at: www.reading.ac.uk/internal/staffportal/news/articles/spsn-855646.aspx (accessed 10 December 2021).

University of Reading (nd) About Us. [online] Available at: www.reading.ac.uk/about.aspx (accessed 10 December 2021).

Amanda Millmore

Amanda Millmore is an Associate Professor in Law at the University of Reading. A former practising barrister, she now teaches criminal, family and tort law and is School Director of Academic Tutoring in the School of Law, with responsibility for leading tutoring and pastoral care for students. Amanda was a member of the Academic Tutor System steering group, working on the project to improve tutoring at Reading and Chair of the university-wide community of practice for Directors of Academic Tutoring when the project was implemented. She has presented this project at various sector-wide conferences.

Dr Jo Cordy

Jo Cordy has been an Academic Developer in the Centre for Quality, Support and Development (CQSD) at the University of Reading since 2017. Prior to that she worked as a Researcher Developer, following a period of post-doctoral research in biochemistry. Jo was the CQSD lead for the Academic Tutor System project, and was responsible for designing and creating many of the staff-facing resources and guidance. Since the end of the project, Jo provides ongoing support and development for academic tutors, and supports the Directors of Academic Tutoring Community of Practice.

Jess Johnson

Jess Johnson is a Strategic Project Manager in the Planning and Strategy Office at the University of Reading. A qualified teacher and experienced project manager, she now leads the design and delivery of institutional strategic projects to enhance teaching and learning and improve the student experience at Reading. Jess managed the strategic project to review the Personal Tutor System and introduce the Academic Tutor System, including facilitating extensive staff and student consultation and working collaboratively with the steering group to support the introduction of the new system.

Cindy Isherwood

Cindy Isherwood has worked in higher education for 20 years across a range of roles in support of teaching and learning. Cindy began her university career in undergraduate admissions and programme management and went on to work in the Vice-Chancellor's Office at the University of Reading where she was Personal Assistant to the Pro-Vice-Chancellor (Teaching and Learning) for 11 years. After a short break, Cindy returned to Reading and took up a role in quality assurance. Most recently, Cindy was the Project Officer for the implementation of the Academic Tutor System project.

Ed White

Ed White was Education Officer and a Director of Reading University Students' Union in 2017. He ensured the student voice was at the heart of proposed changes or policy decisions, and completed a manifesto focusing on improving the academic experience of students. Following this, as Evaluation and Impact Project Officer, he was responsible for implementing a systematic, institutional approach towards evaluation of teaching and learning. Ed received a University Collaborative Award for his contribution to a project raising the profile of student voice and partnership, and gained a Higher Education Academy Associate Fellowship. Ed is now a Quality Enhancement Advisor at London South Bank University.

Lillie-Mae Firmin

Lillie-Mae Firmin was Education Officer for Reading University Students' Union (2018–19). As Education Officer, Lillie-Mae worked closely with students and staff at the University of Reading to improve the student experience. During her time in office, she worked in partnership with the university to support the introduction, delivery and evaluation of the Academic Tutor System, helping to ensure students benefit from the support available. Further highlights include running campaigns on the BME attainment gap and organising the student submission for the TEF subject-level pilot. After graduating in 2020, she is now a civil servant in the Department for International Trade.

Fifi Bangham

Fifi Bangham took up the post of Education Officer at Reading University Students' Union in June 2019. She worked with university staff to implement improvement to the student academic experience, and worked to represent students on university committees. After leaving the Education Officer role, Fifi worked on the design of a new extenuating circumstances procedure within the university. Fifi is now a Year Two teacher at a primary school in West Reading.

Professor Orla Kennedy

Orla is Teaching and Learning Dean with responsibility for student achievement, alongside working with the Schools of Biological Sciences; Chemistry, Food and Pharmacy; and Psychology and Clinical Language Sciences to lead the enhancement of teaching and learning and the student experience. She co-chairs the University Committee on Student Experience and Development, and is the teaching and learning lead for the university's work on academic tutoring, health education, employability and student voice. Orla joined the University of Reading in 2005 and was appointed to the Dean role in 2015 and a Personal Chair in Public Health Nutrition in 2017.

Case study 16

What do the students think? Evaluating academic advising across an institution using the Listening Rooms method

Helen Parkin, Emma Heron and Melissa Jacobi

Themes	Page number locations in the companion book
Developing a sense of belonging among students	13
Differentiating by individual student needs	108–14
Group personal tutoring and advising	114–17
Research and evaluation	4, 12, 175–98
Student involvement and co-creation	61, 107, 116, 167–8
Supplementary support for personal tutoring and advising	22

Introduction

This case study provides an overview of how the Listening Rooms method was used to evaluate the implementation, delivery and impact of academic advising (AA) from both an individual (student voice) and an institutional (recommendations for future practice) perspective. We conducted Listening Rooms with 46 students (23 pairs) to understand student experiences of AA as part of continually enhancing practice.

Eighteen academic departments had two pairs of students talking about their personal experiences of AA. The data generated was shared between key stakeholders across the institution who had the ability to effect change. This case study provides evidence of the impact of AA on individual students through the sharing of their conversations. It also demonstrates how institutions can work with authentic student voices to bring about improvements in delivery.

Academic advising at Sheffield Hallam University

Sheffield Hallam University (SHU) is a large higher education institution in the north of England with over 30,000 enrolled students over three colleges. SHU is relatively unusual in the UK higher education sector in utilising the term academic advising (rather than personal tutoring). It does so to provide a clear remit and focus for advisors in terms of their primary responsibility being to support their students' academic development and progression. Personal issues (or pastoral care) are supported by student support advisors as part of our Student Support Triangle, which sees all students being allocated to, and supported by, three named advisors as follows:

- an academic advisor to support academic progression, personal development and professional development;

- a student support advisor to support pastoral care and welfare concerns;

- an employability advisor to support job searching and career planning.

The Listening Rooms method

With its award-winning approach (Guardian University Awards, 2020) to listening and analysing student experience, the Listening Rooms method, which is uniquely utilised at SHU as an evaluation tool, was applied to our work around AA between September 2020 and January 2021. Two key tenets drive the work: firstly, the fundamental importance to us of evaluating AA through student lived experience and secondly, our commitment to bringing about meaningful change based on genuine student voice data, read and digested by AA staff. The Listening Rooms method is based on the importance of data collection acquired through friendship pairs undertaking a guided and recorded conversation, unsupervised by a researcher, in a private space where they are free to share their feelings. This is an approach which maximises the closeness and trust between the pair by eliminating any 'intervention' from a researcher (Heron, 2020).

Data analysis is undertaken through our Round Table Analysis method, whereby key stakeholders with AA experience and an ability to bring about institutional change share data and reach key recommendations about how advising can be improved across the institution. This is done through a collaborative thematic discussion based on themes emerging from the data and the priorities of the group. Our key stakeholders for analysis included Heads of Teaching and Learning, the Head of Academic Advising, and a senior researcher. Both data collection and analysis have been undertaken remotely using Blackboard Collaborate for data collection and Zoom for the analysis. Both tools have closely replicated the face-to-face experience for participants and stakeholders.

Informed by literature (Heron, 2020), we decided on the following key themes for the students to discuss as these proved useful when reflecting on the support and guidance provided by their academic advisor: self-awareness, achieving, becoming, belonging, happiness and success. Students were asked to find a friend who would also be willing to participate and invite them to a Collaborate session. Once in the Collaborate room, the pair worked their way through a PowerPoint presentation, which guided the conversation. The transcribed conversations were distributed among key stakeholders who read their allocation of anonymised data prior to coming together via Zoom. Stakeholders identified, through the structured thematic discussion online, key success factors and agreed a set of recommendations.

Student perspectives

At SHU, delivery of AA in departments is varied and this is reflected in the friendship conversations undertaken during this research. What is consistent throughout the data is that the AA relationship is valued and appreciated by our students.

Theme 1: relationships

AA is most successful when there is a good relationship between the academic advisor and the student. Thomas and Hixenbaugh (2006, p 6) identified that '...*relationships are central to students' higher education experience and that personal tutors can play an important role in enhancing academic relations*'. We concur and further argue that where good relationships existed, students experienced an increased sense of belonging and felt cared for by the university (see also Thomas, 2012).

> *It almost feels like she's fighting for your professional career... There's no teacher/ student relationship there, it's – I don't want to say a friend but it does feel like a friend in a sense. (Transcript 7)*

> *I do still feel like I belong... I don't feel like I'm just a name in a list. (Transcript 9)*

> *[The academic advisor] put a lot of effort into bonding us all... We weren't just there to do work; she'd put her back into making us all feel loved. (Transcript 10)*

Academic advisors provide '*perhaps the only opportunity for all students to develop a personal, consistent relationship with someone in their institution who cares about them*' (Drake, 2011, cited in Grey and Osborne, 2018, p 286). For this reason, continuity of the academic advisor relationship throughout a student's time at university is important.

> *I feel like if you can have that relationship for the whole way through uni it may be even better as well. (Transcript 7)*

Theme 2: model of delivery

Time allowed for delivery of AA is an important factor in considering how it is best delivered. Thomas (2012) found that as well as offering time benefits, group advising sessions have the additional benefits of enabling students to develop peer support relationships. Here, we found that peer relationships fostered during group AA sessions gave an additional benefit of students continuing discussions outside of the formal teaching environment.

> *I feel with a lot of seminars you're not really– like a lot of people just don't talk… Whereas I feel if we did it with our AA Group, I don't feel it would be that awkward because we've all known each other since the beginning. (Transcript 1)*

Where the AA format allows for only one-to-one sessions, some students felt that there was not enough time to fully explore their personal and professional development. Group AA sessions allowed students more time to explore their personal and professional development with their academic advisor and when used alongside one-to-one sessions, this provided students with both the time and the personal relationship with their academic advisor that they desired.

> *I think it's hard because there's not as much interaction as I feel like there should be with an academic advisor. (Transcript 2)*

> *You know when we have those one-to-one sessions, I don't think there's many of them– I think we had about one or two, which they were great, but I just don't think they were enough. (Transcript 9)*

Theme 3: advocacy and support

Many students reported that their academic advisor was an advocate for them and supported them to achieve. This is echoed by Lee and Robinson (2006) who identify that good AA is about enabling students to make the most from their time at university.

> *[AA] will definitely help us be successful in getting placements and by achieving things in the future, whether it be at uni or not. (Transcript 7)*

> *I just like how [the academic advisor] pushes people because she believes in them. She knows what you can do… I suppose because you know that person believes in you and it's like 'wow'. (Transcript 3)*

Academic advisors also acted as an anchor point for students in challenging times, though sometimes students had to reach out for help first. Morey and Robbins (2011, cited in Grey and Osborne, 2018) propose that established relationships with an academic advisor gives students the confidence to approach a familiar member of staff for help when it is needed.

> *I had a meeting with her the other week and I just felt like– afterwards I felt like a weight was sort of lifted off my shoulder. (Transcript 1)*

> *Well, I called out my academic advisor at one point after I got coronavirus. Basically, saying I need to touch base with you because I'm really far behind on everything. She definitely gave me security. (Transcript 2)*

Institutional perspective: recommendations for future practice

Based on the findings of this research, we have identified the following areas as a priority for development/implementation at SHU to ensure positive staff and student experience of academic advising. These recommendations may be helpful to other institutions dependent on context.

- Students need to feel like they are 'known' as an individual and that there is consistent support available throughout their academic journey.

- It is a priority to ensure that academic advisors understand the remit and importance of the role through training to support the development of strong advisor–student relationships.

- Wherever possible, the academic advisor relationship should be established in the first year and continue through to the end of the students' university journey.

- Delivering a mixture of one-to-one and group AA sessions will optimise the students' experiences of AA.

- AA should not be a standalone function; it should be seen as underpinning the holistic student journey and consideration should be given to how to support other aspects of the student experience.

- Provide space for continued use of Listening Rooms to support continuous improvement.

Conclusion

The Listening Rooms method provides institutions with in-depth insights into student experiences of AA. Students value AA and benefit from strong relationships with their advisors. From a SHU perspective, the recommendations for future practice identified above (already evident and applied in some areas) will now be an expectation for all departments to ensure a consistency of student experience.

Critical reflections

1. To what extent are student views and feedback used to inform developments to:
   - your own personal tutoring practice?
   - your department's personal tutoring practice?
   - your institution's personal tutoring practice?

   What more could be done to improve this?

2. In your specific context, evaluate whether you feel it is preferable to allow a separate specialised role to support students' pastoral care.

3. Explain three strategies to ensure your students don't feel like 'just a name on a list'.

References

Grey, D and Osborne, C (2018) Perceptions and Principles of Personal Tutoring. *Journal of Further and Higher Education*, 44(3): 285–99.

Heron, E (2020) Friendship as Method: Reflections on a New Approach to Understanding Student Experiences in Higher Education. *Journal of Further and Higher Education*, 40(3): 393–407.

Lee, B and Robinson, A (2006) Creating a Network of Student Support. In Thomas, L and Hixenbaugh, P (eds) *Personal Tutoring in Higher Education* (pp 83–90). Stoke-on-Trent: Trentham Books.

Guardian University Awards (2020) Student Experience: Award Winner and Runners-up. [online] Available at: www.theguardian.com/education/2020/nov/25/student-experience-award winner-and-runners-up (accessed 10 December 2021).

Thomas, L (2012) *Building Student Engagement and Belonging in Higher Education at a Time of Change. Final Report from the What Works? Student Retention and Success Programme.* [online] Available at: www.heacademy.ac.uk/sites/default/files/resources/What_works_final_report.pdf (accessed 10 December 2021).

Thomas, L and Hixenbaugh, P (2006) *Personal Tutoring in Higher Education*. Stoke-on-Trent: Trentham Books.

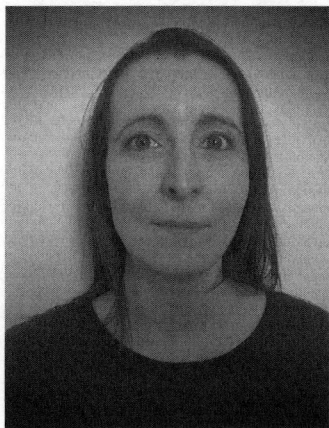

Helen J Parkin

Helen Parkin is a Senior Lecturer in Research, Evaluation and Student Engagement. She is responsible for conducting research into and evaluation of student experience and engagement across the institution. She has led the evaluation of the senior tutor role and implementation of academic advising at Sheffield Hallam University.

Emma Heron

Emma Heron is the Head of Teaching and Learning Enhancement in the College of Social Sciences and Arts at Sheffield Hallam University. Her portfolio covers teaching quality, student engagement and academic advising and she co-leads Listening Rooms across and beyond the institution. Emma has achieved the CRA/SEDA Professional Development Award in Personal Tutoring and Academic Advising and is working on becoming a Recognised Leader in Advising through the UKAT Professional Recognition Scheme.

Melissa Jacobi

Melissa Jacobi is the Head of Academic Advising at Sheffield Hallam University and is responsible for the strategic leadership of academic advising across the institution. Melissa is the membership and onboarding lead for UKAT, has achieved the CRA/SEDA Professional Development Award in Personal Tutoring and Academic Advising as well as the Recognised Leader in Advising through the UKAT Professional Recognition Scheme. Her background is as an academic member of staff teaching sport business management in the Academy of Sport at Hallam.

Case study 17
A framework for personal tutoring: system and activity

Stephen Powell and Alicia Prowse

Themes	Page number locations in the companion book
Boundaries between roles	53–73
Coaching	15–21, 136–52
Differentiating by subject area	–
Framework of personal tutoring and advising	23–5
Institutional review and implementation	23–5
Research and evaluation	4, 12, 175–98
Student involvement and co-creation	61, 107, 116, 167–8
Transition	105–8

Introduction

In this case study we describe an institutional initiative to develop a personal tutoring framework for Manchester Metropolitan University (Manchester Met) as part of a Higher Education Funding Council for England (HEFCE) funded project from 2017–19. The project was undertaken by a central academic support unit and was directed towards undergraduate students across the university.

Through this work, it was apparent that there was a significant amount of dissatisfaction with the effectiveness of existing approaches to personal tutoring (PT) expressed by academics and managers in different forums. At our university, PT is delivered by academic staff, largely through a professional model (Laycock, 2009) where extensive central services are provided to signpost to. Reflecting on our many conversations with staff and students, we caricatured the poorer experiences of personal tutoring as 'Two people in a room that neither wants to be in for a purpose that is unclear to both' – this was our motivation to develop a more effective and personalised approach to PT.

The argument for a reconceptualisation of the relationship between teachers and students is made by Bovill (2020), informed by the work of Biesta (2006), and proposes the relationship between learners and educators to be one of co-creation based on needs, rather than what they see as a commodification model. In our work, we set out to create the structural conditions that would enable ownership of the design and organisation of contextualised approaches to PT at a departmental level, as opposed to a centralised set of prescriptive requirements. This aimed to enable the development of purposeful and caring relationships between the tutor and tutee inspired by a relational pedagogical approach that *'takes seriously questions of trust, recognition and respect which lie at the heart of the student's experience'* (Murphy and Brown, 2012, p 633).

Soft Systems Methodology: a structured inquiry process

We used Soft Systems Methodology (SSM) (Checkland and Poulter, 2006) as an approach to change which can be broadly thought of as a form of participatory action research (known as learning cycles). Like all forms of action research, through a structured inquiry process, those involved are seeking to bring about changes for improvements to identified issues or opportunities. The five learning cycles were:

1. finding out about the activities of PT across the university;
2. identifying the purpose of PT and developing suggested ways in which it could work in an improved manner;
3. holding structured discussions with stakeholders to develop an accommodation of views about desirable changes;
4. defining actions that need to be taken to improve the situation;
5. undertaking ongoing critical reflection as the practitioners using SSM to refine thinking and actions around our intervention.

Using Soft Systems Methodology we learnt that...

Building on our previous investigation's findings, in total 130 students contributed to short interviews and a further ten students were recruited and paid to undertake in-depth reflection and fact finding from fellow students. Staff views were gathered through the established faculty education committee structures to find out about different approaches to PT and share proposals for evaluative feedback from across faculty.

It was apparent from our inquiry that there are a wide variety of approaches to PT but that the purpose was often unclear and poorly articulated. Often, purpose was conflated with the activity of meetings between tutors and tutees and thus the rationale, or *why*, of PT was inexplicit. Without a clear articulation of the purpose, PT becomes a hard 'sell' to tutors and students and impossible to evaluate for impact or effectiveness. In addition, PT is often seen as the solution to a myriad of complex higher education challenges, such as progression, employability and differential outcomes, for which it is under-resourced. This lack of clarity about the purpose and role of PT within institutions is also identified by Walker (2020) with the role considered to be a low-status activity that personal tutors feel neither equipped for nor sufficiently work-loaded to undertake (University of Warwick, 2017, p 27).

Through our inquiry, we identified the following three facets of a fruitful relationship that can make students feel supported, motivated, and sometimes inspired.

1. The tutor cares about me.
2. The tutor helps me improve my work.
3. The tutor values me as a learner.

We also found that students can identify when the personal tutoring offer is insincere; this could be because staff are not committed to the role or because it is under-resourced relative to its stated aims (Prowse et al, 2020). It follows that although we can confidently assert that good personal tutoring is valuable, as Yale (2017) points out, experiencing poor personal tutoring may well be worse than experiencing none whatsoever.

This learning led us to develop the Manchester Met Personal Tutoring Framework

Synthesising the learnings identified in the previous section, we identified a way forward for a personal tutoring framework that allowed for design and implementation choices to be taken as close to the activity of personal tutoring as possible. At the same time, we also put in place monitoring arrangements that would allow for the university to have confidence that effective PT was taking place.

This approach is supported by systems thinking where the principle of self-organisation by those tasked with the implementation is better for addressing the challenge at hand rather than a top-down, '*distant from the activity*' direction (Seddon, 2008, p 82). To achieve this, we promoted thinking about the design of a *system* of personal tutoring as separate from the *activity* of personal tutoring. This allows for appropriate evaluation mechanisms that distinguish between the system and the delivery of PT.

The system of personal tutoring

In line with SSM methodology, a high-level statement for the purpose of personal tutoring was developed:

> *Facilitate students' personal development and academic progress, achievement, career readiness, aspirations, and transitions into and out of university education over time, by encouraging the formation of purposeful relationships with clear boundaries, between students and academic staff, to help students to navigate their own pathways towards autonomy and success.*
>
> (Manchester Metropolitan University, 2019).

To support staff in undertaking the design, implementation and evaluation of PT, a set of resources and accompanying workshops are delivered centrally and presented as a Design Wheel (Figure 17.1).

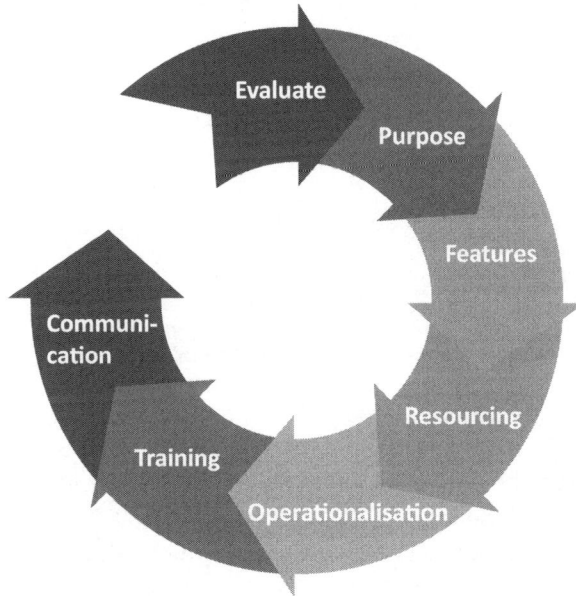

Figure 17.1 *Design wheel*
(Manchester Metropolitan University, 2019)

Indicative explanations of the different wheel components are described below.

1. Evaluate – methods by which data can be collected to evaluate the effectiveness of PT systems.

2. Purpose – a starting point for developing a PT system.

3. Features – components that might make up a PT system such as skill development, finding a Student Union club; goal setting for academic progress; autonomy and career planning, etc.

4. Resourcing – which staff will be involved in personal tutoring, what will the tutor/tutee ratios be, are there ancillary support services that form part of the resource?

5. Operationalisation – who/what role will take overall responsibility for managing and developing the PT system?

6. Training – identification of training that will be required to support staff in the implementation of a PT system.

7. Communication – how will the purpose and operation of your PT system be communicated to students and staff?

The activity of personal tutoring

Once a personal tutoring system is designed, the focus shifts to the role of the personal tutor in implementing it. Broadly, we identified the use of a coaching approach for tutor–tutee meetings as aligning well with the relational pedagogy identified earlier and the intended purpose of PT stated above – in particular, the outcome '*to help students to navigate their own pathways towards autonomy and success*' (Manchester Metropolitan University, 2019).

As a way of capturing the broad intentions of PT, we recognised that the focus of activity can be presented as the 3Cs.

1. **Course**-focused support for academic progress.

2. **Community** building through encouraging participation in a learning community and signposting to support services when required.

3. **Career** planning support towards an identified career path.

This high-level description was developed from what students and staff reported as the essential elements of PT meetings while at the same time allowing flexibility for localised interpretations. However, the real value came as a rhetorical device when explaining to academic staff the role of the personal tutor and how it might vary over time and between meetings with different tutees. Its simplicity and clarity cannot be underestimated as an aid to socialising the underpinning philosophy of PT.

Impact of the Manchester Met Personal Tutoring Framework

At the institutional level, this project was followed by a subsequent initiative to introduce a five-year plan (5YP) across the institution for all students, with the primary intervention being through personal tutors. As part of this work, a baselining of PT was undertaken approximately 12 months after the Personal Tutoring Framework was adopted where 62 staff were interviewed. It was reported to the University Academic Board (July 2020) that there was good uptake of the use of the 3Cs across the institution and that the Personal Tutoring Framework had been broadly welcomed. In addition, centralised communications to students about their time at our university are now framed around the 3Cs for clarity of messaging.

Conclusion

Evaluating this project in cycle five of the SSM has led us to identify some lessons learned. Firstly, in a large university, the implementation of personal tutoring as a *one approach fits all* is unlikely to be effective for the diverse student body that it would be applied to. Instead, empowering local ownership, decision making and accountability is more likely to lead to the development of effective and responsive personal tutoring experiences for students.

Secondly, by separating the design of a system of personal tutoring from the activity of PT, it makes it easier to evaluate the former and implement improvements, rather than conflate with the activity or delivery of PT. The delivery will be varied depending upon the personnel involved and environmental factors such as the value placed on the activity by the institution.

Thirdly, there is value in devices such as the 3Cs: Course, Community and Career in socialising the key ideas of an institution's philosophical approach to PT.

Lastly, using Soft Systems Methodology as an explicit and robust change theory gave us structure, rigour and credibility with our inquiry, countering the feeling of imposition from the centre, which can improve engagement and involvement.

Critical reflections

1. If a new and desired aim of personal tutoring within your department was 'Two people in a room that both want to be in for a purpose that is clear to both', identify as many:

    • driving forces (positive forces to achieve this change) as you can;

    • restraining forces (obstacles to achieve this change) as you can.

2. If you were creating the 'conditions for the ownership of the design and organisation of personal tutoring at department level', create a mind map which details what you feel the necessary conditions would be.

3. For each of the three identified facets of a fruitful personal tutoring relationship (below), identify personal tutoring activities which would help these to be realised.

    • The tutor cares about me.

    • The tutor helps me improve my work.

    • The tutor values me as a learner.

References

Biesta, G J J (2006) *Beyond Learning: Democratic Education for a Human Future*. London: Paradigm Publishers.

Bovill, C (2020) *Co-Creating Learning and Teaching: Towards Relational Pedagogy in Higher Education*. St Albans: Critical Publishing.

Checkland, P and Poulter, J (2006) *Learning for Action: A Short Definitive Account of Soft Systems Methodology and its Use, for Practitioners, Teachers and Students.* Chichester: John Wiley and Sons Ltd.

Laycock, M (2009) *Personal Tutoring in Higher Education – Where Now and Where Next? Literature Review and Recommendations.* SEDA Specials, 25. London: Staff and Educational Development Association.

Manchester Metropolitan University (2019) *Personal Tutoring Framework.* [online] Available at: www.mmu.ac.uk/about-us/professional-services/uta/teaching/personal-tutoring (accessed 1 May 2021).

Murphy, M and Brown, T (2012) Learning as Relational: Intersubjectivity and Pedagogy in Higher Education. *International Journal of Lifelong Education,* 31(5): 643–654.

Prowse, A, Vargas, V and Powell, S (2020) Design Considerations for Personalised Supported Learning: Implications for Higher Education. *Journal of Further and Higher Education,* 45(4): 497–510.

Seddon, J (2008) *Systems Thinking in the Public Sector: The Failure of the Reform Regime... and a Manifesto for a Better Way.* Axminster: Triarchy Press.

University of Warwick (2017) *University of Warwick – Personal Tutoring Review 2017 (PTR 2017).* [online] Available at: https://warwick.ac.uk/services/dean-of-students-office/about/ptr_2017_report_-_final_may_2018.pdf (accessed 1 May 2021).

Walker, B W (2020) Tackling the Personal Tutoring Conundrum: A Qualitative Study on the Impact of Developmental Support for Tutors. *Active Learning in Higher Education.* [online] Available at: https://doi.org/10.1177/1469787420926007 (accessed 14 January 2022).

Yale, A T (2019) The Personal Tutor–Student Relationship: Student Expectations and Experiences of Personal Tutoring in Higher Education. *Journal of Further and Higher Education,* 43(4): 533–44.

Dr Stephen Powell

Stephen Powell is the Associate Head of the University Teaching Academy at Manchester Metropolitan University, where he is responsible for taught provision and the UKPSF recognition scheme for academic staff. He has worked in education for over 30 years, initially as a teacher in the compulsory school sector, and then in higher education. He has particular experience in curriculum design and development. He has developed and managed numerous projects in higher education, working with colleagues to develop new taught provision and improve institutions' educational systems and processes using action research and systems thinking approaches.

Dr Alicia Prowse

Alicia Prowse gained a PhD in Plant Ecology in 2001 looking at the ecological impact of an invasive 'alien' species (Himalayan Balsam) on native plant communities in the UK. She has worked as a university lecturer, woodland surveyor, professional actor and teacher for English to speakers of other languages. She has taught ecology and biology to BSc Biology students; research methods for biologists and social science students, and environmental science and biology to further education students. She has recently retired from the University Teaching Academy at Manchester Metropolitan University. Her research interests are interdisciplinary collaboration, student motivation and academic staff development.

Case study 18
Using Social Identity Mapping in personal tutorials to aid students in their transition and social integration into and throughout higher education

Ian Pownall and Alison Raby

Themes	Page number locations in the companion book
Differentiating by individual student needs	108–14
Embedded into teaching	22
Faculty/school/department-level perspective	23
Student engagement	44, 56, 57, 58–60, 66–7
Supporting student populations	75–85
Transition	105–8

Introduction: the problem

Acculturation of students to higher education and their integration into the social system of a university is their first step in developing academic skills and voice (Aoyama and Takahashi, 2020), contributing to successful transition to higher education (Lochtie et al, 2018). The motivation of the new learner is intrinsically linked to their context and to potentially evolving contradictory identities (Hashimoto, 2002) which can, through dissonance, result in negative coping behaviours as students physically and cognitively distance themselves (Bjork et al, 2020). This was the starting point for our pilot development of Social Identity Mapping (SIM) at the Lincoln International Business School (LIBS) during 2020–21. We will build on this feasibility exploration to develop a wider evaluative framework.

Our objective was to surface and support the development of a socially integrated learner, particularly the new international student (who may feel more inclined to discard unique aspects of themselves) (Bjork et al, 2020), by valuing their social location. Following Sfard and Prusak (2005), we define a learner's social location as the cognitive co-ordination of these identified identity organisations that learners hold views and feelings about. The personal tutor can support the construction of this location.

The context

LIBS operates a hybrid model of Earwaker's (1992) professional and integrated curriculum models where students are referred to central services for certain issues and integrated personal tutoring sessions are also timetabled (McIntosh, 2018). In LIBS, undergraduate students complete group tutorial sessions four times annually with one-to-one meetings also encouraged.

Core concepts

Organising bespoke tutor groups for international students can offer benefits (Lochtie, 2016; Raby, 2020) but is at risk of a deficit view by participants and tutors (Smit, 2012; Page and Chahboun, 2019). An integrated provision was offered where all new international students joined tutee groups to encompass an understanding of academic and social interactions for all students. Exposure to diversity leads to positive coping changes in development and cross-cultural adjustment, such as information seeking, relationship building and positive thinking (Hashimoto, 2002; Portes et al, 2007; Mesidor and Sly, 2016). Support to develop student academic self-efficacy is an established approach to promoting engagement (Zimmerman et al, 1992; Lochtie et al, 2018) and our aim was to develop resources to allow students to identify and academically value their social location (Lochtie et al, 2018).

Supporting student progression through to graduation is one of the greatest delights of teaching (Lochtie et al, 2018). SIM was developed to support effective progression (building on work from Ng et al, 2018 and Cruwys et al, 2016) so students can better manage their academic lifecycle as their social context, motivation and identities evolve (Morgan, 2012; Aoyama and Takahashi, 2020). SIM supports the development of identified factors of student resilience and autonomy extending beyond induction into their programme and social experience. By enabling reflective analysis of the learner's social context, a dialogue between students and tutors results in effective coping and adjustment strategies as students seek to engage more effectively in their new environment (Harmon-Jones, 1999; Cooper, 2019). Multiple group memberships (MGM) are sources of comfort, identity, security and resilience (Sønderlund et al, 2017; Ng et al, 2018). Supporting students through dialogue, enabled by SIM, can help in managing commitments and developing coping strategies, contributing to a transition pedagogy for personal tutors (Lochtie et al, 2018).

Description

The SIM resource comprised an introductory identity discussion, a Qualtrics survey and Excel workbook (coding adapted from Duggirala, 2014). The survey tasked students to identify between seven and 20 groups they felt had significance to their social world. They ranked groups by time, how they felt about that group and that group's capacity to support their studies. Finally, it explored group compatibility from the perspective of influencing and supporting engagement with their studies. Data was combined (following Cruwys et al, 2016) and imported into individual workbooks to generate an interactive visual map of their group memberships. This invoked discussions between student and tutor regarding those groups' impact on their capacity to study, ability to identify with their learning environment and their sense of engagement.

Data gathered

As a pilot project, SIM was optional for use in personal tutorials. Some tutors presented SIM in group sessions before inviting individual completion of the survey. Approximately 30 students chose to participate with some sharing their outputs (used here as illustrative examples). Therefore, while data is limited, we believe there is scope to develop this in future iterations with wider curriculum integration.

We share below one example (Figure 18.1) from a UK first-year student and some of the resulting observations. Solid lines are strong influences, while dotted lines are weaker. Students can select a node from which to view the map dynamically (for example, parents are highlighted below).

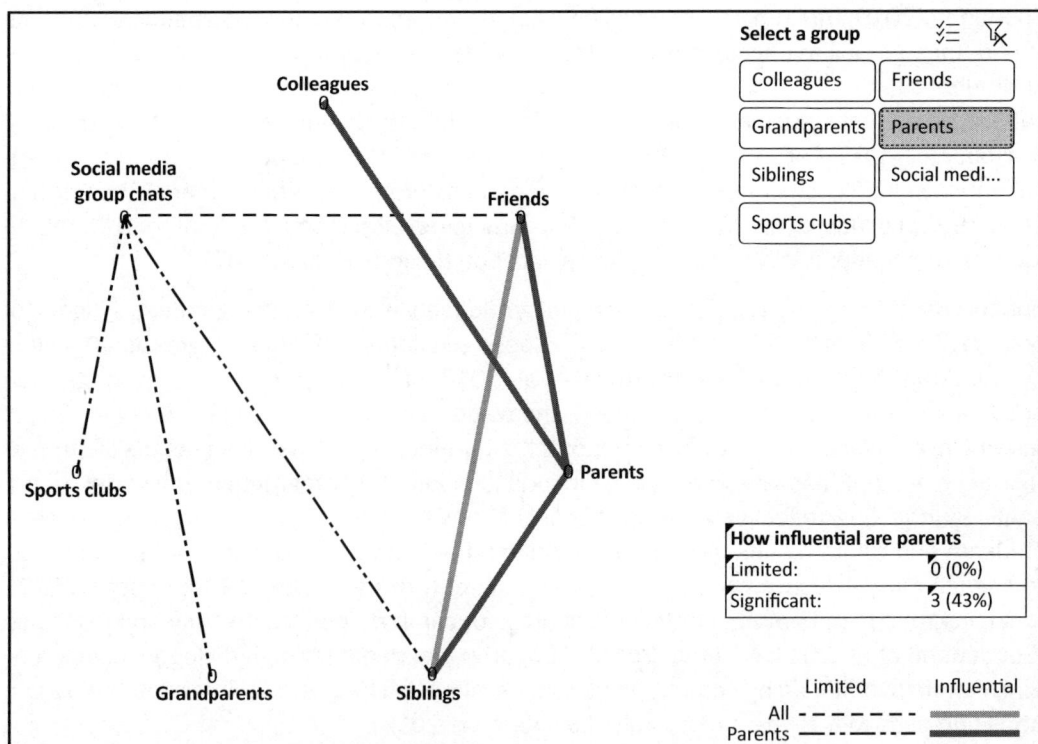

Figure 18.1 Example of a social identity map

Initial SIM observations

- A limited number of network influences were identified overall. We asked the student if there was scope to develop this (their MGMs) to support emergent resilience.

- We asked the student to consider why academic staff were not valued, encouraging the student to reflect upon this through a discussion of the value of communication with their programme leader as they progress towards a professional role.

- Relationships between the friends, parents and siblings were important with close, influential, supportive familial and friendship groups.

- The sports club was unconnected to other parts of their social map. The student commented this was an 'escape' from the academic learning environment (a positive coping strategy) but was mindful of the time it occupied.

- The social media group showed a strong influence generally with friends supporting and engaging with active communications.

Evaluation

The students we interviewed regarded the activity as helpful, pushing them to consider their social world more explicitly, who they were within it and their changing learning context. The illustrative examples use SIM as a structured tool enabling students to reflect upon social location, facilitating an awareness of their change and transition. One comment from a self-identified working-class student was that SIM helped to identify loss between their pre- and post-higher education social context through changing friendships. This had not been anticipated and support was offered. Thinking about friendship groups post-graduation was also identified as important and something not previously considered.

Another participant, a Muslim male, discussed his Muslim friends and recognised how they encouraged and supported each other by sharing experiences of studying and rewarding themselves on completion of tasks. He identified strong links with parents in his home country, reporting to them regularly, and a strong relationship with academic staff, whom he felt free to message to ask for help (particularly during the pandemic). He felt the activity helped him to identify how people and environments affect his study and allowed him to consider how he managed competing demands across his social location while also deriving motivation from within his peer group.

Conclusion

The primary goal was to surface and support the development of a socially integrated learner, particularly in relation to international students who may find higher education transition more challenging. SIM could be particularly beneficial in one-to-one tutorials, in which student and tutor can discuss the issues surfaced by creating the map. It can give tutors more insight into students' identities, helping them to get to know each other more effectively and so they can differentiate the support they provide according to the individual. This listening and communication can form a basis for a more trusting longer-term relationship with tutees (Lochtie et al, 2018).

From the examples cited, surfaced practices are identified by the students that help frame and contextualise their engagement in their learning environment. This can impact on their motivation or support understanding of discord and difficulties in their effective engagement in learning. Difficult conversations can sometimes occur, for example, if the student recognises that some connections may not be beneficial to their settling in at university and studying.

After reviewing the sample maps shared and speaking with the students, our small-scale pilot suggests that SIM can aid student transition by surfacing issues such as managing lost relationships, forging new relationships, cultural time demands and motivational sources. It helps students articulate the discord between 'hidden' aspects of their engagement and their social learning environment through developing critical reflective skills. We believe that SIM can be used to encourage tutees to engage individually with personal tutors, recognising the value of difficult conversations, where tutors support open dialogue, resulting in appropriate structured student support and action plans. Our next step is to expand the scope of the project and develop an evaluative framework through concepts explored in the pilot and constructs from Kang et al (2005) and Sfard and Prusak (2005) regarding cognitive conflict in learners in new supported higher education contexts.

Critical reflections

1. Do you feel the use of Social Identity Mapping (SIM) could support personal tutoring at your institution? If yes, how? If not, why not?

2. If you do not have access to SIM tools (or similar), what strategies could you still implement to gain comparable benefits?

3. If you were looking to implement a new initiative or additional element to personal tutoring practice at your institution, how would you approach piloting and evaluating it?

References

Aoyama, T and Takahashi, T (2020) International Students' Willingness to Communicate in English as a Second Language: The Effects of L2 Self-Confidence, Acculturation, and Motivational Types. *Journal of International Students*, 10(3): 703–23.

Bjork, C, Abrams, A, Hutchinson, L S and Kyrkjebo, N I (2020) "Don't Change Yourselves": International Students' Concepts of Belonging at a Liberal Arts College. *Journal of International Students*, 10(3): 553–70.

Cooper, J (2019) Cognitive Dissonance: Where We've Been and Where We're Going. *International Review of Social Psychology*, 32(1): 1–11.

Cruwys, T, Steffens, N K, Haslam, S A, Haslam, C, Jetten, J and Dingle, G A (2016) Social Identity Mapping: A Procedure for Visual Representation and Assessment of Subjective Multiple Group Memberships. *British Journal of Social Psychology*, 55: 613–42.

Duggirala, P (2014) Mapping Relationships Between People Using Interactive Network Chart. [online] Available at: https://chandoo.org/wp/network-relationship-chart (accessed 10 December 2021).

Earwaker, J (1992) *Helping and Supporting Students: Rethinking the Issues*. Buckingham: Society for Research into Higher Education and Open University Press.

Harmon-Jones, E (1999) Toward an Understanding of the Motivation Underlying Dissonance Effects: Is the Production of Aversive Consequences Necessary? In E Harmon-Jones and J Mills (eds) *Cognitive Dissonance: Progress on a Pivotal Theory in Social Psychology* (pp 71–99). Washington, DC: APA.

Hashimoto, Y (2002) Motivation and Willingness to Communicate as Predictors of Reported L2 Use: The Japanese ESL context. *Studies in Second Language Acquisition*, 20(2).

Kang, S, Scharmann, L C, Noh, T and Koh, H (2005) The Influence of Students' Cognitive and Motivational Variables in Respect of Cognitive Conflict and Conceptual Change. *International Journal of Science Education*, 27(9): 1037–58.

Lochtie, D (2016) A 'Special Relationship' in Higher Education? What Influence Might the US Higher Education Sector Have in Terms of Support for International Students in the UK? *Perspectives: Policy and Practice in Higher Education*, 20(2–3): 67–74.

Lochtie, D, McIntosh, E, Stork, A, and Walker, B W (2018) *Effective Personal Tutoring in Higher Education*. St. Albans: Critical Publishing.

McIntosh, E (2018) The 4 Step Tutorial Pathway – A Model of Early Intervention & Transitional Support (EI) to Facilitate Resilience and Partnership Working in Personal Tutoring. Paper presented at the *UK Advising and Tutoring (UKAT) Conference*, 27 March 2018, Derby.

Mesidor, J K and Sly, K F (2016) Factors that Contribute to the Adjustment of International Students. *Journal of International Students*, 6(1): 262–82.

Morgan, M (2012) *Improving the Student Experience: The Practical Guide for Universities and Colleges*. London: Routledge.

Ng, N W K, Haslam, S A, Haslam, C and Cruwys, T (2018) 'How Can You Make Friends If You Don't Know Who You Are?' A Qualitative Examination of International Students' Experience Informed by the Social Identity Model of Identity Change. *Journal of Community and Applied Social Psychology*, 28: 169–87.

Page, A G and Chahboun, S (2019) Emerging Empowerment of International Students: How International Student Literature Has Shifted to Include the Students' Voices. *Higher Education*, 78: 871–85.

Portes, P, Sandhu, D, Nixon, C B, Moreno, D Arcila, J and Matthews P H (2007) The Cultural Adaptation and Adjustment Scale (CAAS): A Multidimensional Approach to Assessing Ethnic and Gender Social Identities. Centre for Latino Achievement and Success in Education (Working Paper). [online] Available at: https://esploro.libs.uga.edu/esploro/outputs/report/Clase-working-paper-The-cultural-adaptation-and-adjustment-scale-CAAS-A-multidimensional-approach-to-assessing-ethnic-and-gender-social-identities/9949316501802959 (accessed 18 December 2021).

Raby, A (2020) Student Voice in Personal Tutoring. *Frontiers in Education*, 5: 120.

Sfard, A and Prusak, A (2005) Telling Identities: In Search of an Analytic Tool for Investigating Learning as a Culturally Shaped Activity. *Educational Researcher*, 34(5): 14–22.

Smit, R (2012) Towards a Clearer Understanding of Student Disadvantage in Higher Education: Problematising Deficit Thinking. *Higher Education Research & Development*, 31: 369–80.

Sønderlund, A L, Morton, T A and Ryan, M K (2017) Multiple Group Membership and Well-Being: Is There Always Strength in Numbers? *Frontiers in Psychology*, 8: 1038.

Zimmerman, B J, Bandura, A and Martinez-Pons, M (1992) Self-Motivation for Academic Attainment: The Role of Self-Efficacy Beliefs and Personal Goal Setting. *American Educational Research Journal*, 29(3): 663–76.

Dr Ian Pownall

Ian Pownall is an Associate Professor at Lincoln International Business School. He has previously worked at Chester Business School (Programme Leader) and Hull Business School (Director of Learning and Teaching). Ian's background is in the pure sciences before moving into politics and then business. He has interest in how students engage in higher education, especially international students.

Alison Raby

Alison Raby is a senior lecturer, senior tutor and programme leader at Lincoln International Business School. She previously worked at Nottingham Trent International College, teaching international students preparing for university. Prior to that, Alison was a teacher of English as a Foreign Language and ran an English school in Poland. She completed a Master's in Education with the Open University, where she studied applied linguistics, and specialised in analysing the academic writing of Chinese students. Alison is working on a PhD (Professional) in Education around personal tutoring and Chinese students. She is Social Media and Publicity Officer for UKAT.

Case study 19
Personal tutoring as a USP: what happens when personal tutoring is made a priority?

Jennie Robinson

Themes	Page number locations in the companion book
Centralised model	21–2
Embedded into teaching	22
Pastoral support	21–2, 56
Research and evaluation	4, 12, 175–98
Role types – expert versus generalist; senior and specialised personal tutor and advisor	22–3
Transition	105–8

Introduction

Fresh, holistic tutoring models are exciting, but do they work long term? This case study reviews the effects of implementing a centralised tutoring model and analyses the sustainability of the scheme.

In 2012, I joined Leeds University Business School (LUBS) as a whole-cohort personal tutor, tasked with making personal tutoring 'front and centre' for students and the department, and instigating an accompanying compulsory module. The school sought to make expert, targeted, consistent personal tutoring a unique selling point (USP) for the business manage-ment course. The aim was to improve recruitment, retention, attainment and student satis-faction on the programme (Watts, 2011; Grillo and Leist, 2013).

The scheme had already run for a year as a successful pilot with a colleague taking the first cohort. As she moved into the second year with her students, I took on the next cohort, who I tutored through to graduation. I took on 35 students, all with three A grades at A level or equiva-lent, mostly domestic (only four international students) and evenly balanced for gender. This case study is a personal reflection on how the centralised tutoring module was implemented and developed over the years, and its long-term impacts, benefits and challenges.

Overview

The LUBS vision was that students would have the same specialist personal tutor supporting them throughout their degree. This would ensure consistency for students, while 'freeing' other staff from personal tutoring. The model aligned with, and had the advantages of, the centralised 'super tutors' model described by Stork and Walker (2015) with the addition of a compulsory first-year module led by the tutor supporting transition and reflection.

This context reflected an acknowledgement that the existing tutoring system was not working to best effect. It was a traditional system (Stork and Walker, 2015) with all staff asked to tutor, whether or not it was their choice or forte. The feeling was that students experienced variable support, which held down National Student Survey (NSS) results and recruitment; however, this was anecdotal rather than empirical since communications were sporadic.

The primary goal was to improve the student experience and thereby recruitment, which school leads insisted was required in order to keep the degree viable. Moving tutoring wholly to staff motivated towards it, and away from staff who were not, created a secondary goal of improving staff contentment. In turn, this would benefit students as non-tutoring staff were able to direct more energy into research-led teaching (Schertzer and Schertzer, 2004).

The project

The scheme LUBS instigated had two elements: the centralised 'super tutor' (Stork and Walker, 2015) and the creation of a personal tutoring-oriented taught module.

The tutor

The specialist personal tutor was, specifically, enthusiastic and skilled in pastoral care, know-ledgeable about the university's support systems and where to refer students in difficulty, well versed in personal development and employability teaching, and amply rewarded for the role (constituting half a full-time workload). This allowed time and space to develop and main-tain university networks, to spend enough time with each student to develop knowledge and trust, and to monitor students' progress across their other modules. The tutor stayed with their tutees through the programme, returning to become first-year tutor when their cohort graduated. The tutor was the first face students saw during induction, a regular contact through teaching and meetings in each academic year, accompanied students to disciplinary meetings or prize-givings, and was there at graduation to cheer their students' achievements. The aim was to give students an unobtrusive but constant, supportive presence and a clear point of contact in any emergency. Many students fed back that they valued that sense of support, even if they hadn't used it, and parents reported reassurance in having an identifiable, consistent staff member responsible for students' well-being, which in some cases had encouraged parents to influence their child in favour of choosing our course (Nora, 2004).

The taught module

The compulsory level 1 module had activities and content on academic transition in the first semester and employability skills in the second (Picton et al, 2021). A weekly seminar with the tutor allowed a relaxed atmosphere to develop, gave a weekly 'check-in' opportunity to resolve minor issues and kept personal tutoring 'front of mind' for students. The module encouraged engagement with workshops, placements and summer activities, creating a sense that personal development was built into the degree. It also boosted our employability statistics and improved student confidence. There was a marked jump in Destination of Leavers from Higher Education (DLHE) scores when the first 'new model' cohort graduated; after being stuck at 82 per cent for several years up to and including 2014–15, we jumped to 92 per cent in 2015–16. We have built on this since and are currently at 99 per cent.

Evaluation and reflection

Our hope that improved student experience would attract more applicants was realised which enabled us to grow the degree and to recruit more tutors. The intake in 2013–14 was 57 (compared to 35 in 2012–13 in my cohort), rising to around 100 in 2014–15. The intake is now consistently around 170–180 per year. Consequently, we now employ three tutors per year cohort, each staying with their own group throughout their university journey. Increased student numbers demanded, and paid for, the additional tutors.

A welcome by-product of the scheme was improvement in staff–student communications. Many extra improvements arose through listening and learning from students. Regular contact allowed me to hear from all my students (not just the most engaged or the most panicked) about their lived experience of the degree. For example, students let me know that feedback on their coursework from other modules was highly variable. I raised this gently in a staff meeting and discovered in turn a lack of confidence in some staff, who asked for support with giving effective feedback. I put on a workshop showcasing good examples of feedback and giving tips on how to formulate useful advice. This was well attended and I continued it in subsequent years. The NSS result for feedback averaged 46 per cent in 2012; the following year's cohort averaged 58.5 per cent. Today our average for this score is 74 per cent. The impact of the tutoring model is primarily on student support, but there is secondary impact in allowing us to resolve issues in other aspects of their experience (Gibbons et al 2015).

Legacy and future

Grey and Osborne (2018) note the currency of comparing tutoring models and outcomes as institutions in the UK and worldwide continue to review their practices (Hunte et al, 2020;

Picton et al, 2021). Nine years' experience of a 'super tutor' system (Stork and Walker, 2015) has given us a rare length of perspective on the impact of the scheme, which is useful to share.

We have learnt that it works very well indeed with multifactorial benefits that snowball. In fact, a long-term outcome has been resourcing issues: my first intake of 35 students became 175 after five years of the scheme. Of course, we are delighted that students are enjoying their time with us and finding the system effective; this success obliged us to hire more tutors, as noted, but also meant that more staff were needed throughout the degree. In theory, this cycle pays for itself and could continue indefinitely, but there are 'knock-on' effects, such as a shortage of rooms for personal tutor meetings, cohorts becoming too large to bond and lecture theatres being too small to house the cohort in a single session, creating minor diseconomies of scale.

Cohort increase was gradual over the first five years and was capped when we reached 175, where it has been for the past four years. Increasing recruitment created a virtuous circle with 'word of mouth' promoting further increase, an effect which amplified over successive years. The biggest increase point occurred after the pilot cohort completed the NSS, as this was the first opportunity for official, rather than informal, reviews of the student experience. However, another corollary of our better communication was learning how much applicants trusted informal review websites more than the official websites. Programme directors adopting this scheme should commit to a complete cohort cycle to see the full benefit, although immediate benefits will also arise.

Conclusion

Our tutoring model became a significant, though not isolated, element in our 'cocktail' of recovery (Burnes, 2004, p 989). While it is not possible to 'prove' that the improvements claimed in this case study arose directly from the tutoring model, there is close alignment based on my experience, conversations and feedback from different stakeholders.

Our conclusion is that giving tutoring a high profile in student timetables and staff workloads, a consistent, identifiable and skilled tutor, and a structure of low impact but persistent delivery, improves the student experience and in turn reaps reputational and income benefits. I personally learnt that effective tutors are not just supporters of, but conduits between students, their teachers and policy makers (Yale, 2019).

> ### *Key messages*
>
> • Appointing a person who values personal tutoring is vital.
>
> • Tutoring should be in the academic timetable – if it's not scheduled, students see it as lesser.
>
> • Students are happier to attend personal meetings and speak openly within them when tutors are familiar from regular teaching.

- Tutors need to communicate, act on, and feed back on insights gained from tutees.
- Every student in the year should get the same service, availability and support.
- Beneficial effects amplify over time in a virtuous circle.

No model is without its downsides. Moving all tutoring to specialists meant colleagues sometimes fell out of touch with student-related policies. However, colleagues benefitted from increased student numbers, better communications, and improved engagement and attendance on modules resulting from our pastoral support.

I believe that our tutoring model has had a positive impact on students and has enabled our degree to thrive. The module plus 'super tutor' model is relatively simple but its compound benefits are many.

Critical reflections

1. Can anyone be an effective personal tutor? Should all academics be personal tutors? Consider the arguments for and against.

2. Identify the advantages and disadvantages of adopting a centralised personal tutoring model for:

    - the student;

    - the specialist personal tutor and those academic staff now not performing the personal tutor role;

    - the department/faculty or institution.

3. Thinking about the institution or department you work in, what do you feel the reaction would be from key stakeholders to the suggestion of adopting a centralised personal tutoring model and why? If you already use this model, would you suggest it to others and why?

References

Burnes, B (2004) *Managing Change*. Harlow: Pearson Education Limited.

Gibbons, S, Neumeyer, E and Perkins, R (2015) Student Satisfaction, League Tables and University Applications: Evidence from Britain. *Learning and Individual Differences*, 37: 210–16.

Grey, D and Osborne, C (2018) Perceptions and Principles of Personal Tutoring. *Journal of Further and Higher Education*, 44(3): 285–99.

Grillo, M C and Leist, C W (2013) Academic Support as a Predictor of Retention to Graduation: New Insights on the Role of Tutoring, Learning Assistance, and Supplemental Instruction. *Journal of College Student Retention: Research, Theory & Practice*, 15(3): 387–408.

Hunte, A, Khan, W Z and Maharaj, R (2020) An Evaluation of a Pilot Study of the Personal Tutoring Programme in Improving Skills Development at the University of Trinidad and Tobago. *International Journal of Higher Education*, 9(1): 280–91.

Nora, A (2004) The Role of Habitus and Cultural Capital in Choosing a College, Transitioning from High School to Higher Education, and Persisting in College Among Minority and Nonminority Students. *Journal of Hispanic Higher Education*, 3(2): 180–208.

Picton, C, Jaquet, A and Bell, C (2021) *Enhancing Student Success Through an Advising Curriculum.* [online] Available at: https://unistars.org/papers/STARS2021/06D.pdf (accessed 22 October 2021).

Schertzer, C B and Schertzer, S M (2004) Student Satisfaction and Retention: A Conceptual Model. *Journal of Marketing for Higher Education*, 14(1): 79–91.

Stork, A, and Walker, B (2015) *Becoming an Outstanding Personal Tutor: Supporting Learners through Personal Tutoring and Coaching.* St Albans: Critical Publishing.

Watts, T E (2011) Supporting Undergraduate Nursing Students Through Structured Personal Tutoring: Some Reflections. *Nurse Education Today*, 31(2): 214–18.

Yale, A T (2019) The Personal Tutor–Student Relationship: Student Expectations and Experiences of Personal Tutoring in Higher Education. *Journal of Further and Higher Education*, 43(4): 533–44.

Dr Jennie Robinson

Jennie Robinson has been a university teacher and personal tutor for 20 years, with roles including Programme Director, Director of Student Education, and Dissertation Leader. She co-founded the teaching innovation group at Leeds University Business School, is a theme leader for a cross-university initiative, and was a commissioner and diversity lead for the Commonwealth Scholarships. Personal tutoring has been a constant role throughout, and is the most rewarding, challenging and fun part of her professional life.

Case study 20
Professional large group mentoring as an alternative to the 'traditional' personal tutoring system

Dorottya Sallai

Themes	*Page number locations in the companion book*
Differentiating by subject area	–
Group personal tutoring and advising	114–17
Pastoral support	21–2, 56
Programme perspective	24, 45–6
Research and evaluation	4, 12, 175–98
Role types – expert versus generalist; senior and specialised personal tutor and advisor	22–3
Transition	105–8

Introduction

In my case study I will reflect on how the newly introduced large group mentoring system within the management department at the London School of Economics (LSE), a member of the Russell Group, impacted the student experience on the BSc Management programme. The case study will shed light on the way large group mentoring and student support is designed in terms of organisational structure and how the roles are defined and shared within the mentoring team. The case study is based on my personal and professional insights gained through working in small group-based tutoring systems, as well as in a large group system, where a small group of professionals cover the personal tutoring of a whole under-graduate programme. My case study will showcase the differences between the two systems from an organisational point of view and walk the reader through how the new solutions introduced at the LSE – which may be considered an innovation in UK higher education – have made an impact on the student and staff experience.

History and context of personal tutoring within the management department at the London School of Economics (LSE)

Large group mentoring had been introduced at the LSE's management department as an innovative way to improve the student experience. The 'traditional' organisational arrangement of personal tutoring originated from *the 'in loco parentis'* tutor system of Oxford and Cambridge (Earwaker, 1992), where tutors provided pastoral care for their students in groups of 11 to 15 (Lochtie et al, 2018). Our department decided to change this approach. The new system integrates academic and pastoral support and is delivered by a team of four professionals (who are allocated at least 50 per cent of their time for mentoring) for all the students on the BSc Management programme.

As with many innovations, the new system was triggered by a necessity. The management department's National Student Survey (NSS) scores – which measures undergraduate student satisfaction of the BSc Management programme – had been relatively low since the UK's Teaching Excellence and Student Outcomes Framework (Department for Education, 2017) was introduced in 2017.

According to the department's survey in 2016, undergraduate students felt that they do not receive enough support and attention from their personal tutors and the quality of the tutoring relationship was dependent on the academic tutor's personality and priorities. Indeed, not all tutors are well equipped to address the needs of students whatever their background (McFarlane, 2016). The experiences of students at LSE were in line with findings of earlier studies which claimed that changing student expectations related to the drastic increase in tuition fees in the UK, rising student numbers leading to challenging staff–student ratios (Grey and Osborne, 2018), and resulting in a situation in which both students and staff were unhappy and unable to meet each other's needs. We needed to find a way to improve the student experience while also creating more realistic expectations for faculty members who felt overwhelmed by the amount of academic and pastoral issues they were required to manage as personal tutors of undergraduate students.

Large group mentoring as an alternative practice

The introduction of the new system was phased in gradually over three years. First in 2017, LSE introduced a new structure of mentoring in which first-year students were allocated to one professional mentor, while second- and third-year students – who were still mentored by faculty members in small groups – were offered two meetings per term with their personal tutor. Although these changes led to some improvement, the dual challenge of students needing more specialised and accessible academic and pastoral support, and staff's inability to provide this support due to time constraints, pressures on research outputs and lack of training, has not been resolved.

The complexity of mentoring

Our institutional practice suggested that while postgraduate students require less personal, pastoral and progress-related support, those studying for their first degree need guidance and care on multiple interdependent areas. The lack of congruence between what is expected from the role and what is experienced by the student can lead them to having strong negative emotions (Yale, 2020), which may lead to low NSS outcomes. After identifying the complexity of the issue, the management department decided to restructure its personal tutoring system. The department introduced a new structure for personal tutoring at the undergraduate level and – along with LSE's new institutional approach – rebranded it as 'academic mentoring'.

Large group mentoring in practice

Large group mentoring refers to the nature of the role: instead of allocating 11 to 15 students to an academic, four mentors cater for a large cohort of 150–200 students in each year group. The programme has approximately 500 students enrolled overall.

Table 20.1 *Staff responsibilities*

Year group BSc in Management programme	Mentor role	
Year 1	Academic/pastoral mentoring provided by one mentor (professional services staff)	
Years 2 and 3	Academic mentoring provided by: • one academic for second-year students; • another academic for third-year students.	Pastoral mentoring provided by professional services staff for both second- and third-year students.

Table 20.1 shows staff responsibilities. The two academics are both on the education career track. The team's roles and responsibilities are divided along clearly identified boundaries, which makes the management of issues transparent and easy to communicate to the students.

Mentoring for first-year students is based on the pastoral model (Grey and Osborne, 2018) whereby students are advised by one person on academic and personal matters (Lochtie et al, 2018). Students transitioning from secondary schools and colleges go through an adaptation or a sense-making process (Yale, 2020) and therefore need pastoral and academic support at the same time. It is beneficial if this support is provided by the same person since the nature of the challenges that students are facing may overlap the boundary of academic and personal issues. In the second and third years, however, most students will be able to identify whether they require academic or pastoral support. In these year groups the academic side of mentoring includes all areas related to progress and learning, while the pastoral side of mentoring relates to personal challenges, attendance, well being, stress and anxiety or being referred to other university services.

Roles and responsibilities of academic mentors

Allen and Smith have identified five domains in which quality advising contributes to student development as outlined below.

1. *'Integration of the student's academic life and career goals with each other and the curriculum and co-curriculum'*

2. *'Referral to campus resources for academic and non-academic problems'*

3. *'Provision of information about degree requirements, policies and procedures'*

4. *'Individuation, or consideration of students' individual characteristics'*

5. *'Shared responsibility',* to help students become responsible for their own education.

(Allen and Smith, 2008, p 609)

Applying Allen and Smith's framework (2008), I illustrate below how the role of academic mentoring is divided along roles and responsibilities, some of which are distinct, whereas others overlap (see Table 20.2). The overlap in roles shows that mentors need to work closely together to meet students' needs.

Table 20.2 *Roles and responsibilities of the academic mentor team – for second- and third-year undergraduate students*

Allen and Smith's five domains of student development (2008, p 609)	Responsibility within the team		Rationale
Integration	Academic mentor		The academic mentor has a better understanding of the curriculum, academic sessions and how these link with career pathways

Table 20.2 (Cont.)

Allen and Smith's five domains of student development (2008, p 609)	Responsibility within the team		Rationale
Referral		Pastoral mentor	The pastoral mentor has a broader understanding of the student's personal needs and university services
Provision of information	Academic mentor (course choice, help with interruptions, resits, inclusion plan, deferrals, degree classification)	Pastoral mentor (administrative issues such as attendance monitoring, keeping in touch with unregistered students, referrals to services)	Shared between academic and pastoral mentors depending on the type of information
Personalisation	Academic mentor	Pastoral mentor	Both mentors through one-to-one meetings
Shared responsibility for their own education	Academic mentor	Pastoral mentor	Both mentors through one-to-one, mini-group and group sessions

(Based on Allen and Smith's (2008) framework)

To provide continuity of personal relationships with the students, the academic members of the mentoring team teach all incoming first-year students on one of their core modules and then start mentoring them in their second year.

Evaluation, impact and outcomes

Based on student feedback and the substantial improvement in the NSS results, the large group mentoring system has been positively received by the student body. The scheme was phased in from 2017–18 and became fully functional by 2019–20. Compared to 2015–16, seminar attendance for first-year students increased from 82 per cent to 91 per cent in 2017–18. Students also showed increased academic attainment in first-year quantitative courses such as statistics and mathematics. In 2016–17, 19 per cent of students achieved a first in maths, in 2017–18 this increased to 34 per cent, while in statistics 47 per cent of the students achieved a first compared to 27 per cent a year earlier. While not directly attributable to large group mentoring these are indicative of the positive improvements in students' progress.

Furthermore, the department's NSS results have increased from 64 per cent in 2018 to 79 per cent in 2019 and 85 per cent in 2020. Satisfaction with academic support increased from 62 per cent in 2018 to 68 per cent in 2019 and 81 per cent in 2020 (when the scheme became fully functional for all year groups). Satisfaction with learning resources increased similarly from 67 per cent in 2018 to 81 per cent in 2020.

Conclusion

Although the system is new and hence long-term impacts are not measurable yet, it is evident that students on the undergraduate programme are happier with the support they receive today than they were a few years ago.

Key messages

The key messages regarding large group mentoring from this case study are as follows.

- As the needs and skills of undergraduate students evolve, during their first year and beyond, the support provided should also.

- Second- and third-year students can better identify whether they require academic or pastoral support, so the two can be more separated and specialised.

- The division of mentoring tasks along academic and pastoral lines makes responsibilities transparent, tasks manageable for staff and a reality which more closely matches expectation.

- Large group mentoring, led by more closely specialised mentors, can positively affect the student experience by increasing student satisfaction and progress.

Critical reflections

1. From your own experience as a personal tutor and as a student, analyse whether you believe it is possible and desirable to effectively dissociate academic and pastoral support. If this approach is adopted, what key factors would need to be considered to ensure it is effective?

2. Devise two feasible strategies to ensure your practice is personalised to address individual student needs.

3. Even if academic staff do not undertake a designated personal tutoring role but continue to teach or work with students individually, identify the key personal tutoring skills, behaviours and values which will enhance their educational practice.

References

Allen, J M and Smith, C L (2008) Faculty and Student Perspectives on Advising: Implications for Student Dissatisfaction. *Journal of College Student Development*, 49(6): 609–24.

Department for Education (2017) *Teaching Excellence and Student Outcomes Framework Specification.* [online] https://assets.publishing.service.gov.uk/government/uploads/system/uploads/atta chment_data/file/650179/Teaching_Excellence_and_Student_Outcomes_Framework_specif ication.pdf (accessed 10 December 2021).

Earwaker, J (1992) *Helping and Supporting Students: Rethinking the Issues.* Buckingham: Society for Research into Higher Education and Open University Press.

Grey, D and Osborne, C (2018) Perceptions and Principles of Personal Tutoring, *Journal of Further and Higher Education*, 44(3): 285–99.

Lochtie, D, McIntosh, E, Stork, A and Walker, B W (2018) *Effective Personal Tutoring in Higher Education.* St Albans: Critical Publishing.

McFarlane, K J (2016) Tutoring the Tutors: Supporting Effective Personal Tutoring. *Active Learning in Higher Education*, 17(1): 77–88.

Yale, A (2020) What's the Deal? The Making, Shaping and Negotiating of First-Year Students' Psychological Contract with Their Personal Tutor in Higher Education. *Frontiers in Education* 5: 60.

Dr Dorottya Sallai

Dorottya Sallai is an Assistant Professorial Lecturer in the Department of Management at the London School of Economics and Political Science (LSE). Her work is published in peer-reviewed journals such as the *Journal of International Management, Business and Society* and the *Journal of Common Market Studies* (JCMS). Her book chapter on multinationals' non-market strategies was published by Palgrave Macmillan. She is a Senior Fellow of the Higher Education Academy and Founding Chair of the Women and Gender Forum at the Society for the Advancement of Socio-Economics (SASE). Dr Sallai has provided consulting and research for governments, companies, non-governmental organisations (NGOs) as well as the European Commission.

Case study 21
Moving from distributed to centralised academic advising: making the case for change

Susan Smith

Themes	Page number locations in the companion book
Centralised model	21–2
Faculty/school/department-level perspective	23
Institutional review and implementation	23–5
Role types – expert versus generalist; senior and specialised personal tutor and advisor	22–3
Supporting student populations	75–85

Introduction

This case study illustrates an innovative approach to academic advising (often also referred to as personal tutoring) devised and implemented at the University of Sussex Business School. It outlines the problems encountered with the prior distributed academic advising model, the evaluation of a range of alternative approaches and how a business case was constructed to form a centralised group of academic success advisors. This group of academics is fully focused on academic advising and reflects the importance placed on the support offered to students through this activity and its influence on student retention and success. Now two years into a three-year pilot, the initial feedback is positive.

Overview of the University of Sussex Business School

The University of Sussex Business School offers a range of undergraduate and taught masters courses to students studying on campus. There are approximately 4500 on-campus students studying at the school of which approximately 78 per cent are undergraduates. The student body is diverse, both in terms of nationality as well as prior experience of education.

In common with most UK universities, undergraduate academic advising was distributed across all faculty with everyone allocated a student load and related workload time. While originally students were matched to members of faculty likely to teach on their degree, this was not always possible as student numbers grew. For postgraduate students, the course directors were expected to take on the advising role and for those managing large courses this created significant additional work.

Limited formal guidance or training was provided, leading to expressions of concern that they did not feel fully prepared for the role (Yonker et al, 2019). Overall, the student experience of academic advising was variable (Holland et al, 2020) with students making unfavourable comparisons between faculty members. This is reflected in the literature which links disappointment with academic advising to broader dissatisfaction measures (Vianden, 2016).

The centralised academic success advisors are academic members of staff who are fully focused on academic advising in recognition of the professional demands of the role (McGill, 2019). They are similar in some ways to the primary role advisors found predominantly in the USA (Walker, 2020), although in this example they are employed on academic contracts.

Student academic success advisors

To address ongoing weaknesses in National Student Survey (NSS) outcomes for the student support dimension, combined with a persistent low level of student engagement with the academic advising process, we conducted an evaluation of the existing academic advising model. The evaluation identified significant variability in the student experience. Variability included the perceived boundaries of the role by both students and faculty, and the some-what transactional nature of interactions where students sought references. Furthermore, we found that because academic advising was a small part of each academic's overall role, it often competed with other calls on their time, leading to advising activities becoming marginalised and a perceived lack of availability to students.

We considered a number of options including strengthening the existing model. As a result, we evaluated three potential structures for academic advising: the pastoral model where the tutor offers both academic and pastoral support; the professional model, which focuses on expert staff focused on advising as their primary role; and the curriculum integrated model, which embeds structured group advising sessions into the formal curriculum (Earwaker, 1992). Concurrently, we interrogated the assumption that all academics should be academic advisors (Grey and Osborne, 2018).

The first option considered was to strengthen the existing system through establishing clearer boundaries for academics and investing in a rolling training programme combined with embedding academic advising into the Postgraduate Certificate in Higher Education for new academics and the school induction processes. The accountability for undertaking academic advising would also have been established more formally through using data related to the activity in probation and annual appraisal processes.

The second option we evaluated was to create a specialist team of academic success advisors to provide a consistent contact point and level of service for students. The recording of meetings in a consistent manner across the team was also expected to facilitate interrogation of patterns and lead to timely interventions. For detailed subject-specific advice, students would be directed to the module or course convenor. This did not present a change from the existing situation as departmental academics are not generally experts in all specialisms or course structures.

The proposal involved redistributing the workload time previously devoted to academic advising to fund the new team. Potential drawbacks included the likely fluctuations in work between term time and out of term and the volume of references required from academic advisors as increasing numbers of students apply for postgraduate study (where in most instances two references are required). While students could meet with any advisor they have a named advisor in recognition of the importance of developing a consistent relationship with the students throughout their period of study (Drake, 2011).

The final option we considered was embedding advising into a core first-year module. This would have required significant curriculum change and as such was not a realistic option. Furthermore, it did not address the needs of those joining directly into the second year of some of our undergraduate courses nor the needs of postgraduate students.

We were mindful that the university's vision of the role was focused on student learning (Holland et al, 2020). As a result, the case was made for recruitment of dedicated academics, working in partnership with both professional services colleagues within the school and across the university as well as with discipline-focused academics. The proposal was approved for a three-year pilot which began in 2019–20.

Evaluation, impact and outcomes

The implementation resulted in a number of positive outcomes for students and staff. While initially there was some disappointment from both academic advisors who had undertaken the role in a proactive manner and the students who had benefitted from such advising, the move was welcomed by both faculty and students.

For students, the key outcomes of the change have been as follows.

Visibility

- The team are highly visible within the school both through their physical and virtual presence. They lead sessions at welcome events, attend departmental meetings and report activity to the school's Senior Management Team. This means that students are significantly more aware of the team and the support that they can provide. For example, all students are automatically enrolled on the academic success advisor site in the virtual learning environment (VLE), which contains a range of guidance and resources, along with links to appointment booking and skills development workshops.

Availability

- Appointments can be scheduled in advance via an online booking system. This allows students to book meetings when it suits them rather than being reliant on multiple emails to set up a meeting.
- Drop-in sessions allow students with urgent issues to be seen very quickly.

Responsiveness

- A shared mailbox ensures work is distributed efficiently and that students receive rapid responses to their queries.

For the school, the benefits of the new model of academic advising are as follows.

Transparency

- The impact of academic advising is increasingly transparent and we seek to use a range of measures, both formal and informal, as part of the evaluation process. Data considered includes internal surveys, student feedback and NSS data among others. We are mindful that approaches to the measurement of advising outcomes are often problematic beyond individual cases; however, measures of retention, student success and graduation are typically adopted (Padak and Kuhn, 2009; McGill, 2019). Further data will be available following the third year of operation to facilitate a statistical analysis of retention and success rates of students who have studied under the new arrangement in comparison to those that did not.

Reporting and analysis

- To provide a greater insight into the effectiveness of academic advising we have built a comprehensive reporting system which now enables a monthly dashboard to be created, reporting trends both at a departmental and thematic level, providing improved insight into patterns of student needs throughout the academic year so that we can start to proactively develop interventions. Currently we have nearly two years of data to compare and the average monthly volume of recorded contacts has increased by approximately ×2.4. This type of data analysis was not possible under the prior system where only certain forms of contact were formally recorded, meetings were not clearly categorised by reason and the content of records was not consistent.

While the evaluation and reporting continues to evolve, it has started to address the criticisms related to a lack of visibility of the contribution of academic advising and provides signalling to others that the role is important and valued (Walker, 2020).

Conclusion

The pilot scheme seeks to recognise the professional work of academic advising and unravel the historic bundling of academic advising with other faculty responsibilities (Padak and Kuhn, 2009).

Insights and take-aways include the following.

- The academic success advisors develop an ongoing relationship with students focused on promoting student success throughout their entire learning journey (Vianden, 2016).

- The model has the potential to scale-up across institutions and is transferable to other institutional contexts.

- Further improvements within the Business School are likely to involve both developing the team as individuals and the service that they offer. These activities are expected to be complementary.

  o Aligning advisors to develop specialisms in supporting student success, for example transitions to UK higher education for students entering via articulation agreements (agreements providing students who have completed studies elsewhere a route into an undergraduate degree, for example through direct entry to the second or final year) and support for students of colour.

  o Engaging in scholarship to contribute to shaping the discipline. To date, the team have started to share their work internally at the school's Annual Festivals of Teaching and Learning and externally via UK Advising and Tutoring (Wang et al, 2020).

  o Developing a career path for those involved in academic advising.

  o Supporting achievement of professional recognition through the UK Advising and Tutoring Framework (UKAT, 2019) as a measure of expertise and currency in the field.

As the student intake continues to broaden (in terms of their experience prior to entering higher education) and we enter a post-pandemic environment, there is likely to be a renewed focus on academic advising across the sector. We hope that our experiences changing our school's model of academic advising contribute to the development of academic advising as a critical function in the contemporary university.

Critical reflections

1. How effectively does your department/faculty collect and report on relevant data to evaluate personal tutoring activities? Write down how the impact of personal tutoring could be measured:

    *   by you individually;

    *   by your departmental lead;

    *   by senior managers across your institution.

2. If your department adopted a centralised academic advising model, what personal tutoring specialisms would be most useful for your student cohort and why?

3. The research from Yale and Warren (Case study 25) identifies that personal tutoring practice can differ on the basis of discipline. Do you feel it matters whether a personal tutor is from a similar discipline to their students? Explain your reasoning.

References

Drake, J (2011) The Role of Academic Advising in Student Retention and Persistence. *About Campus*, 16(3): 8–12.

Earwaker, J (1992) *Helping and Supporting Students. Rethinking the Issues.* Buckingham: Society for Research into Higher Education and Open University Press.

Grey, D and Osborne, C (2018) Perceptions and Principles of Personal Tutoring. *Journal of Further and Higher Education*, 44(3): 285–99.

Holland, C, Westwood, C and Hanif, N (2020) Underestimating the Relationship Between Academic Advising and Attainment: A Case Study in Practice. *Frontiers in Education*, 5: 145.

McGill, C M (2019) The Professionalization of Academic Advising: A Structured Literature Review. *NACADA Journal*, 39(1): 89–100.

Padak, G and Kuhn, T (2009) Voices from the Leadership of Academic Advising. *NACADA Journal*, 29(2): 56–67.

UKAT (UK Advising and Tutoring) (2019) The UKAT Professional Framework for Advising and Tutoring. [online] Available at: www.ukat.ac.uk/framework (accessed 1 October 2021).

Vianden, J (2016) Ties That Bind: Academic Advisors as Agents of Student Relationship Management. *NACADA Journal*, 36(1): 19–29.

Walker, B W (2020) Professional Standards and Recognition for UK Personal Tutoring and Advising. *Frontiers in Education*. [online] Available at: https://doi.org/10.3389/feduc.2020.531451 (accessed 14 January 2022).

Wang, H, Sperring, D, Watson, S and McKinney, L (2020) No Student Left Behind. *UKAT – UK Advising and Tutoring*. [online] www.ukat.ac.uk/community/blog/posts/2020/july/no-student-left-behind (accessed 10 December 2021).

Yonker, J E, Hebreard, D and Cawley, B D (2019) Validating Faculty Advising Through Assessment. *NACADA Journal*, 39(1): 34–49.

Dr Susan Smith

Susan Smith is Associate Dean (Education and Students) at the University of Sussex Business School. Susan is a Senior Lecturer in Accounting and a Fellow of the Institute of Chartered Accountants in England and Wales. She has contributed to a number of working parties to further professional development in the accountancy profession, business schools and more broadly across the higher education sector, including a UKAT working party developing professional recognition in academic tutoring. Susan also serves on the Editorial Board of the *Journal of Perspectives in Applied Academic Practice* and as a trustee of UKAT.

Case study 22
Exploring the values of personal tutoring via a level 7 academic practice module

Ruth Clayton Windscheffel

Themes	Page number locations in the companion book
Developing a sense of belonging among students	13
Postgraduate Certificate in Learning and Teaching in Higher Education	4
Problem-based learning	–
Reflective practice	153–67, 170–1
Values in personal tutoring and advising	32–9

Introduction

This case study explores an academic, values-based approach to personal tutor education. It focuses on how I embedded a critical exploration of personal tutoring's core values – as defined by Lochtie et al (2018) – into a 15 credit, level 7 module on student support and personal tutoring.

Context

I teach academic practice at a medium-sized, pre-1992 university in London. It has approximately 20,000 students from more than 150 countries of whom about one-third are postgraduates with a similar split between UK and non-UK students (HESA, 2018–19).

Nearly 60 per cent of UK students are characterised as Black, Asian and Minority Ethnic (BAME) and just over 57 per cent of all students identify as female. The university employs staff from over 75 countries deployed across five academic schools and several professional service sections. No single department is responsible for personal tutoring. The Learning and Development directorate to which I belong maintains a student support information hub, delivers bespoke personal tutor training when requested and teaches the Master of Arts (MA) module 'Student Support and Personal Tutoring' (SSPT). SSPT forms part of our Higher Education Academy (HEA) accredited Postgraduate Certificate in Academic Practice. Typical participants include university staff (new and more established tenured academics, postgraduate researchers who teach, visiting lecturers and professional services staff), staff from other London higher education institutions (HEIs) which do not offer taught teaching qualifications and nurse-educators from local NHS trusts. Since 2017–18, I have been the module lead for SSPT, teaching 96 participants over four consecutive years (cohorts numbering between 14 and 35).

Developing personal tutoring through an academic module

SSPT was designed to deliver information about professional student support services to academics working in a heavily devolved university system. However, module evaluations showed that simple information-giving was insufficient without adequate '*tailoring as to how services available can enhance student support*' (2015–16) and participants requested (again in their module evaluations) a shift to '*stories... of how things are done*' (2016–17).

I immediately introduced a more balanced structure to the module, initially using Earwaker's (1992) model of academic, pastoral and professional student support. I also addressed an overreliance on professional student support staff acting as visiting lecturers, who tended to overemphasise the referral aspect of academics' student support role rather than enabling their own practice. These initial measures influenced the 2018–19 evaluations with participants noting that SSPT was more '*clearly and logically developed*'. However, I recognised that changing colleagues' perception of their role as triaging for the professionals would require more fundamental curriculum review.

We needed to heighten participants' sense of personal investment in personal tutoring. I made extensive use of Lochtie et al (2018); the following insight of theirs proving especially helpful: '*Having the right skills is important to be able to carry out your job, but it is your core values that drive you to take those actions repeatedly*' (p 40). Space was therefore made in SSPT for values-focused critical thinking activities (based on those in Lochtie et al, 2018). These helped participants identify and reflect on their personal core values and how these might be deployed in their academic practice. Opportunities were also afforded for participants to hear how others (peers and visiting speakers) lived out their values through personal tutoring and student support. From 2018–19 we included sessions on compassion, kindness and self-care in the module. This had an instant impact on evaluations. For the first time, participants reported that SSPT had made them '*more reflective*', and they appreciated the '*safe space*' given to them for contemplative and mindful discussions (2018–19), meeting Barnett's requirement that curricula should '*contain sufficient space and spaces, such that "authenticity" and "integrity" are likely to unfold*' (2009, p 438).

Mindful of Biggs' (1999) levels of teaching model and the need to value students as individuals, the module was refocused to engage participants not only with who our students are and what we do as teachers but also what our students do – and feel – in dialogue with those supporting their learning. Student identity formation and belongingness (Thomas, 2012; Thomas et al, 2017) are now key parts of SSPT. The most impactful method we introduced to develop these aspects involved problem-based learning (PBL). Participants work in small groups for their assessment and each group is assigned two simulated 'tutees' for the course of the module. These deliberately diverse 'tutees' are introduced with a short biography and back story before proceeding to send regular messages to their 'tutors' (for example, asking for advice or disclosing problems) via a virtual learning environment forum. The 'tutors' then work together to formulate responses which are discussed in class. Both the tutor feedback and evolving student 'stories' are ipsative (meaning previous issues and advice are deliberately built on and compared) and help participants go beyond theoretical knowledge alone and become effective personal tutors through making decisions in the moment in response to real-life, personalised situations.

The upheaval of the Covid-19 pandemic has intensified this challenge to being and becoming with, for instance, Gravett and Ajjawi (2021) questioning the idea of 'belonging' as a stable category when discussing students and their support. Given such uncertainties, the importance of developing tutors' core values seems even more important. As Barnett (2009) observes, '*working out the connection between knowing and being/becoming requires a thinking through of the kinds of human being that we want our students to become; and that is partly a matter of our value choices*' (p 444).

Assessing personal tutoring

By 2017–18, SSPT's assessment had changed from a 3000-word essay to a group poster assessment. Group work is notoriously challenging (Windscheffel, 2019), but it can nurture resilience, collaboration, mutual respect, generosity and preparedness to listen (Barnett, 2009): all skills necessary for supporting students and personal tutoring. Working and being assessed in teams has provided myriad opportunities for SSPT participants to live out their core values (high expectations, diplomacy and adhering to the '*equal partner, not superior*' approach) and of practising associated skills ('*building rapport*', '*teamwork*', '*decision-making*' and '*problem-solving*') (Lochtie et al, 2018, p 33; pp 39–40). Crucial to enabling this learning is allocating interactive class time to peer-led group work supported by tutor feedback. As the participants have discovered, this work is not always easy and the poster has elicited mixed reactions. Some have found it '*a good way to present*' and '*a new learning experience*' (2018–19). Others have found cooperating with others hard. Each year I have had opportunities to role-model the same values and skills that my participants are developing by undertaking mediation work with teams experiencing pressure and strain.

Conclusion

SSPT is similar to the long-running module I inherited: we still invite external experts to present and to answer participants' questions, and we still direct learners towards relevant university policies and services. However, rather than being a platform to host the performance of professional expertise, the module is now a course of active and individual learning, set within a vital community of academic practice, with the identification and exploration of values and vocation at its heart. Participant feedback and the positive contribution of alumni to personal tutoring in their schools illustrate the benefits of this kind of academic development of personal tutoring. One colleague who undertook SSPT wrote their MA dissertation on personal tutoring and is now a senior personal tutor co-leading a school-based review of the service; they return each year to talk to current participants about their work. The diverse student profiles we use for our PBL activity, which were initially developed collaboratively with the Students' Union and student support services, have, in their current form, been used in an institution-wide forum designed to support staff to engage with who our students are, and gain a greater appreciation not only of the challenges they face but the richness and energy they bring to our community.

Key messages

From my experience of adapting SSPT, I would make the following recommendations to other institutions considering a similar approach.

- Focus on the role of personal tutor not just as a point for referral but as someone who can have an impact on student identity and belonging.

- Structure the course around a relevant model or framework (for example, UKAT, 2019).

- Foreground values through discussion and reflection, providing a safe space to explore issues and empowering participants to decide on their own ideals and ethos.

- Ensure that the assessment is meaningful and linked to participants' practice.

- Embed an emphasis on inclusive practice both to align with the professional values of the UK Professional Standards Framework for Teaching and Supporting Learning in Higher Education (UKPSF) (HEA, 2011) and to support UK HEIs' development of enhanced inclusive learning environments – an effort necessitated by the UK government's 2014 reform of the Disabled Students' Allowance which extended HEIs' anticipatory responsibilities under the 2010 Equality Act (Department for Business, Innovation and Skills, 2014).

- Utilise a group-work approach, whether to organise assessment or in-class activities, but scaffold and support this so that difficult but vital learning can be gained about listening to and supporting others compassionately without judgement.

There is more to do. A recent audit of personal tutoring in my institution revealed significant differences persist between the schools in the way personal tutoring is managed (as is often the case with diffused systems where executive power is delegated rather than held centrally). Of note was a finding which indicates the need to improve the uptake of personal tutor training across the institution given a concern that 'demand' for this was weak and leaving staff potentially unprepared for their roles. Requiring all tutors to undertake an MA module may not be the answer but developing such a module has, I believe, given us a clearer understanding of how participant engagement in, and commitment to, such an endeavour may be gained.

Critical reflections

1. Suggest how your department and institution could increase the demand and accessibility of personal tutoring education. Identify which of these suggestions you could personally influence and how.

2. In addition to the suggestions for using problem-based learning and peer-led group work, suggest other effective learning and teaching approaches, together with a rationale, to help the participants to be an effective personal tutor.

3. Other case studies highlight the importance of understanding your values, beliefs and attitudes for the development of your own practice. Reflect on a specific example of where you have supported a student and the outcome was 'successful'. Create a mind map to identify links between specific impactful things you did or said and the values, beliefs and attitudes which were present.

References

Barnett, R (2009) Knowing and Becoming in the Higher Education Curriculum. *Studies in Higher Education*, 34(4): 429–40.

Biggs, J (1999) What the Student Does: Teaching for Enhanced Learning. *Higher Education Research and Development*, 18(1): 57–75.

Department for Business, Innovation and Skills (2014) Higher Education: Student Support: Changes to Disabled Students' Allowances (DSA). Written Ministerial Statement by David Willetts, Minister for Universities and Science, on Future Changes to Disabled Students' Allowances. [online] Available at: www.gov.uk/government/speeches/higher-education-student-support-changes-to-disabled-students-allowances-dsa (accessed 10 December 2021).

Earwaker, J (1992) *Helping and Supporting Students: Rethinking the Issues.* Buckingham: Society for Research into Higher Education and Open University Press.

Gravett, K and Ajjawi, R (2021) Belonging as Situated Practice. *Studies in Higher Education.* https://doi.org/10.1080/03075079.2021.1894118

HESA (2018–19) Open Data and Official Statistics. [online] Available at: www.hesa.ac.uk/data-and-analysis (accessed 10 December 2021).

Higher Education Academy (HEA) (2011) *UK Professional Standards Framework*. York: Higher Education Academy. [online] Available at: www.heacademy.ac.uk/system/files/downloads/ukpsf_2011_english.pdf (accessed 16 December 2021).

Lochtie, D, McIntosh, E, Stork, A, Walker, B W (2018) *Effective Personal Tutoring*. St Albans: Critical Publishing.

Thomas, L (2012) *Building Student Engagement and Belonging at a Time of Change in Higher Education*. London: Paul Hamlyn Foundation. [online] Available at: www.heacademy.ac.uk/system/files/what_works_final_report.pdf (accessed 10 December 2021).

Thomas, L, Hill, M, O'Mahony, J and Yorke, M (2017) *Supporting Student Success: Strategies for Institutional Change. What Works? Student Retention and Success Programme. Final Report.* [online] Available at: www.advance-he.ac.uk/knowledge-hub/supporting-student-success-strategies-institutional-change (accessed 10 October 2021).

UKAT (UK Advising and Tutoring) (2019) The UKAT Professional Framework for Advising and Tutoring. [online] Available at: www.ukat.uk/professional-development/professional-framework-for-advising-and-tutoring (accessed 1 October 2021).

Windscheffel, R C (2019) Case Study on Posters and Group Work: Diversifying Assessment on an MA in Academic Practice. *Educational Developments*, 20(1): 13–16.

Dr Ruth Clayton Windscheffel

Ruth Clayton Windscheffel is Senior Lecturer in Educational Development at City, University of London, Senior Fellow of the Higher Education Academy and a Fellow of the Royal Historical Society. She module leads on the MA Academic Practice and is Deputy Director of the Higher Education Academy fellowships programme, RISES, at City. Ruth trained as an historian and has worked in UK higher education for more than 20 years, holding a variety of academic and professional roles. Her education and research interests include inclusive practice and student attainment, academic and professional identities, postgraduate researcher education, the affective domain in higher education, student support and personal tutoring.

Case study 23

Student success coaching: developing a model that works to enhance personal tutoring and student success

Arcadia Woods and Ruth Lefever

Themes	Page number locations in the companion book
Boundaries between roles	53–73
Coaching	15–21, 136–52
Developing a sense of belonging among students	13
Student engagement	44, 56, 57, 58–60, 66–7
Student peer support	61, 107, 116
Supplementary support to personal tutoring and advising	22
Well-being	13, 23, 55, 179–80

Background and context

In November 2019, a new professional services advisory role, the Student Success Coach (SSC), was introduced at the University of Bradford (UoB) to support student engagement, progression and success.

The intention was not to target a specific cohort of students or data set (such as poor engagement statistics) but rather to offer an additional form of support for students within a wider suite of student success initiatives, such as academic skills advice and peer assisted learning; one that focused on ongoing individual support and proactive student involvement.

Coaching is an active approach to advising which supports students to seek strategies and solutions for themselves, and has an emphasis on follow up and accountability (McWilliams and Beam, 2013; International Coaching Federation, 2021), as well as signposting/referring students to appropriate specialist support (Pechac and Slantcheva-Durst, 2019). With its individualised, student-centred approach (Robinson, 2015), coaching has been demonstrated to contribute to improved student retention (Bettinger and Baker, 2014) and attainment (Capstick et al, 2019) in higher education. Coaching can also facilitate a relationship between a student and a member of staff who is genuinely invested in their journey (Robinson and Gahagan, 2010), which can be a key contributor to a sense of belonging and student success (Thomas, 2012).

At UoB, students attend coaching alongside personal academic tutor (PAT) meetings and we propose that having a positive advising relationship with the SSC can act as a gateway to a more effective PAT–student relationship and help reinforce the value of personal tutoring. We will explore this through our evaluation, looking at engagement with the offer and through thematic analysis of student and staff experiences of student success coaching.

Implementation of student success coaching

Student success coaching model

We selected the GROW (goal, reality, option, will do/way forward) model (Whitmore, 2002) as the basis for our approach. Although originally developed for management coaching, GROW has been adopted successfully in higher education (Robinson, 2015; Eriksen et al, 2020). Coaching session plans were developed for the first, ongoing and final sessions. Accountability is an important and valuable component of coaching (Robinson and Gahagan, 2010); therefore, each plan begins with reflection on progress since the last meeting. The final session includes a reflection on what the student can take forward to their future studies.

Although we planned to make coaching open to any student, due to the practicalities of having just one staff member, four programmes were identified to offer coaching in the pilot phase (February to August 2020). These reflected a diverse range of disciplines and students.

Due to the resource limitations, students who may need support most were prioritised and suggested reasons to refer students to coaching were developed (low attendance; assessment concerns; challenging circumstances). However, all referrals were made by the programme teams who were free to extend the criteria. Indeed, reasons students were referred were diverse, reflecting the student body and different aspects of the student journey.

Boundaries with personal tutoring

Our aim was that coaching would complement personal tutoring rather than compete with it. In collaboration with programme staff, we established the following boundaries (Lochtie et al, 2018, pp 55–6) between the two staff roles (as opposed to between the staff and students).

Independence

The SSC is independent from the programme team. Students can talk honestly about challenges with their course and choose how much information they share with their PAT.

Expertise

The PAT is still the initial contact for any programme/academic advice. By contrast, the SSC is a professional services role with strong links to other support areas (for example, Counselling and Mental Health, Disability Service). This enables discussion of what specialist support is most appropriate and direct signposting by the coach.

This can also increase the knowledge base of personal tutors about support available from professional services (Walker, 2020).

Time

The PAT–student relationship can last for the student's whole programme, whereas coaching takes place over a discrete time period. However, students can take forward strategies identified to their future studies with the support of their PAT. The reflective conversation in the final coaching session facilitates this.

Evaluation

Evaluation methodology

Evaluation was built into the design of the pilot and comprised three main components. Firstly, engagement with the coaching offer, as illustrated by the number of students and programmes involved in the coaching pilot.

Secondly, student outcomes were assessed using two activities. The first of these was the Well-being and Engagement Framework (WBEF), adapted from Grant (2012), which enabled students to self-assess well-being and engagement with their studies before and after coaching. Case study experiences of coaching were also captured through an email questionnaire.

Thirdly, staff outcomes were assessed through case studies. These were gathered from programme leaders taking part in the pilot phase through an email questionnaire.

Where informed consent was granted, these results are presented below. Three students gave consent for the anonymised WBEF results to be shared. One student and two programme leaders gave consent for their case study questionnaire to be included. Of the students who gave their consent, all had attended at least four sessions.

We acknowledge the limitation of the low numbers included in this analysis; however, this was a small-scale pilot phase project and further evaluation is planned.

A thematic analysis (Coffey and Atkinson, 1996) was undertaken across the evaluation components to develop links, themes and to establish the main findings.

Evaluation findings

Our evaluation indicated that students and staff engaged with the student success coaching offer and had a positive experience of this support.

Engagement was illustrated by the number of students attending coaching and by the number returning to attend multiple sessions. In total, 52 students were invited between February and August 2020. Seventeen students attended at least one coaching session (attendance rate of 33 per cent). Of these, 12 students came to two or more coaching sessions, and four students attended at least six sessions. The uptake rate for this pilot phase was lower than that reported for some larger coaching schemes in the literature (Capstick et al, 2019; Pechac and Slantcheva-Durst, 2019); however, the actual number of students attending was similar to other schemes in their early years of operation (Robinson, 2015).

We identified the following themes capturing experiences and the positive impact of taking part for both students and staff.

Valuing an additional source of support

Both students and staff valued the coaching support offered. Students found the individual support useful and staff viewed it as an important additional resource:

> *I am really grateful that the opportunity of taking part in the student success coaching was presented to me. (Student)*
> *It has been an incredibly valuable resource for the team and students (Staff)*

Increased student engagement

Using the WBEF as a measurement tool, students self-reported an increase in engagement with their studies (Figure 23.1). They also raised benefits, such as improved time management and approach to their studies:

> *I think that I structure my work very differently since starting student success coaching.*

Increased student well-being

Using the WBEF as a measurement tool, students self-reported an increase in well-being after coaching (Figure 23.1). They also expressed positive impact regarding building in time for self-care, which contributed to mental well-being:

> Help is given to better manage time spent doing work in order to allow for some self-care which is so very important for mental well-being.

Coaching also provided an opportunity to refer students to other services, including mental health support, which may have contributed to improvements in well-being.

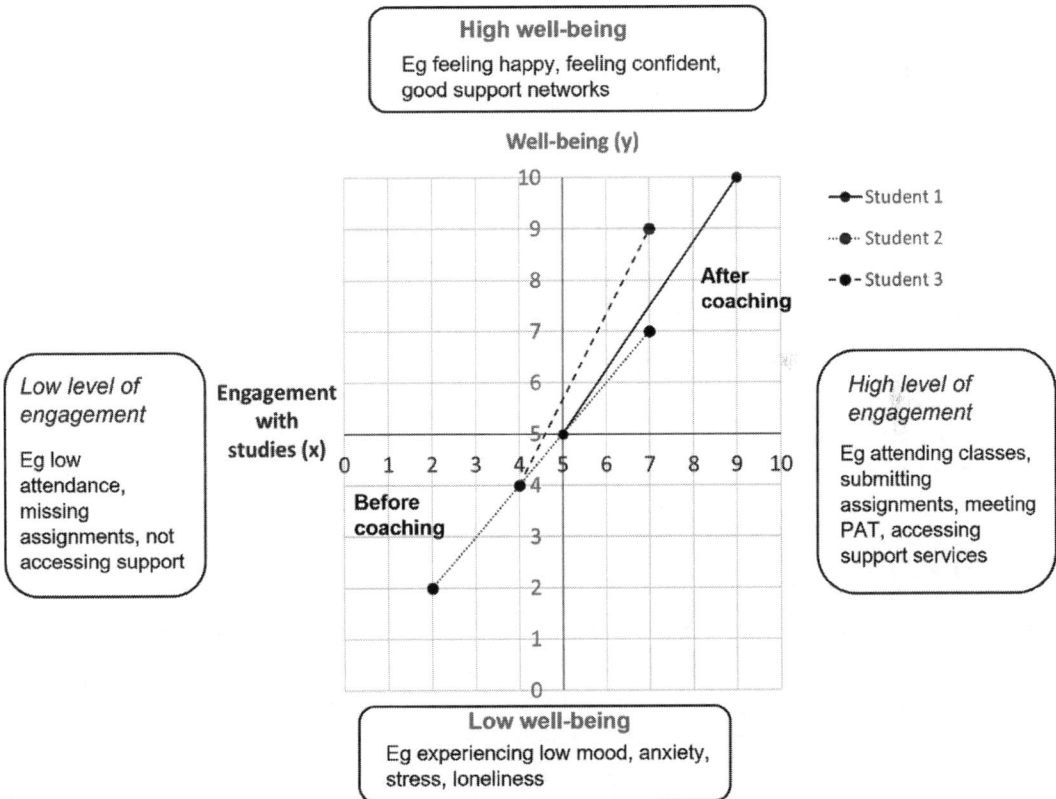

Figure 23.1 *Results of the Well-being and Engagement Framework (WBEF) for three students attending coaching during the pilot phase of the programme (collected from July to November 2020). The WBEF was adapted from Grant (2012) for use in student success coaching.*

The coaching approach

The approach itself emerged as beneficial, notably that it was action based, built independence and offered support from a neutral source:

The action plans we agreed together at the end of each session meant I had a structure to work with. (Student)

Coaching... helps students to identify what they need to do and how to do it without doing it for them or leaving them to sink or swim. (Staff)

Students can... work on areas of weakness and ask 'stupid' questions that they might feel embarrassed about with their PAT. (Staff)

Coaching complements personal tutoring

Our findings implied that coaching complemented personal tutoring and staff did not see it as detrimental to the PAT role. Notably, staff were keen to see the coaching role expanded and used further within the programme:

I would like it to be made more plentiful so that students can make even more use of it.

Value during Covid-19 pandemic and online learning

An unintended outcome was the value of coaching during the pandemic and in supporting online learning in particular. Attendance was not impacted during this time as we saw continued engagement and the ability to develop an effective coaching relationship remotely.

I was able to get support with staying on top of everything... during the Covid-19 pandemic. (Student)

Especially in this age of remote/online learning, my perception is that many students struggle to make the transition to degree level study. (Staff)

Conclusion

We have demonstrated that there is value to an independent advisory role, the Student Success Coach, at the University of Bradford, which can support student success through engagement and well-being. Coaching is a valuable addition to the student support offer, recognising that some students benefit from one-to-one tailored support.

The introduction of coaching has had a positive impact for both students and staff (as outlined in the themes above) and can be seen to complement personal tutoring. From the practitioner perspective, coaching has also facilitated a valuable two-way exchange of knowledge between professional services and academic staff.

Implications for practice

- A model of higher education coaching has been designed and implemented which offers a framework that could be applied at any institution as part of a support offer.
- Coaching in higher education can complement and strengthen personal tutoring rather than compete with it.

- There is value to situating coaching within professional services to offer independent and neutral support that can both improve student access to specialist support and build PAT knowledge of the support landscape.

- A flexible model should be offered with capacity to work online/remotely where needed.

Future work

We are expanding student success coaching to increase the cohort of students taking part across the institution and will also explore opportunities to offer different modes of coaching to students, including self-coaching and peer coaching. We will continue to work with programmes to increase the uptake of student success coaching as the role expands beyond the pilot phase. Rolling out coaching across the institution will enable evaluation involving larger numbers of participants allowing us to understand more about the impact of this support for both students and staff.

Critical reflections

1. If you were leading the implementation of the Student Success Coach model as described in the case study, explain what the role boundaries and communication considerations are to ensure an effective system of support for the students. For each of these, identify who the key stakeholders are who you would need to consult with.

2. Is it useful to inform your students that you will be 'coaching' them? What are the advantages and disadvantages of doing this? Do you feel your students will know what this is and how would you explain it to them?

3. If you accept that coaching students is beneficial for them generally, describe two personal tutoring situations where it may be better not to coach and, instead, to be more directive overall and offer your expertise.

References

Bettinger, E P and Baker, R B (2014) The Effects of Student Coaching: An Evaluation of a Randomized Experiment in Student Advising. *Educational Evaluation and Policy Analysis*, 36(1): 3–19.

Capstick, M K, Harrell-Williams, L M, Cockrum, C D and West, S L (2019) Exploring the Effectiveness of Academic Coaching for Academically At-Risk College Students. *Innovative Higher Education*, 44(3): 219–31.

Coffey, A and Atkinson, P (1996) *Making Sense of Qualitative Data: Complementary Research Strategies*. Thousand Oaks, CA; London: SAGE.

Eriksen, M, Collins, S, Finocchio, B and Oakley, J (2020) Developing Students' Coaching Ability Through Peer Coaching. *Journal of Management Education*, 44(1): 9–38.

Grant, A M (2012) ROI is a Poor Measure of Coaching Success: Towards a More Holistic Approach Using a Well-Being and Engagement Framework. *Coaching: An International Journal of Theory, Research and Practice*, 5(2): 74–85.

International Coaching Federation (2021) Frequently Asked Questions. [online] Available at: https://coachingfederation.org/faqs (accessed 10 December 2021).

Lochtie, D, McIntosh, E, Stork, A and Walker, B W (2018) *Effective Personal Tutoring in Higher Education*. St Albans: Critical Publishing.

McWilliams, A and Beam, L (2013) Advising, Counseling, Coaching, Mentoring: Models of Developmental Relationships in Higher Education. *The Mentor: Innovative Scholarship on Academic Advising*, 15.

Pechac, S and Slantcheva-Durst, S (2019) Coaching Toward Completion: Academic Coaching Factors Influencing Community College Student Success. *Journal of College Student Retention: Research, Theory & Practice*, 23(3): 722–46.

Robinson, C E (2015) *Academic/Success Coaching: A Description of an Emerging Field in Higher Education*. PhD thesis, University of South Carolina – Columbia. [online] Available at: https://scholarcommons.sc.edu/etd/3148 (accessed 10 December 2021).

Robinson, C and Gahagan, J (2010) Coaching Students to Academic Success and Engagement on Campus. *About Campus*, 15(4): 26–9.

Thomas, L (2012) *Building Student Engagement and Belonging in Higher Education at a Time of Change. Final Report from the What Works? Student Retention and Success Programme.* [online] Available at: www.heacademy.ac.uk/sites/default/files/resources/What_works_final_report.pdf (accessed 10 December 2021).

Walker, B W (2020) Tackling the Personal Tutoring Conundrum: A Qualitative Study on the Impact of Developmental Support for Tutors. *Active Learning in Higher Education*. [online] Available at: https://doi.org/10.1177/1469787420926007 (accessed 14 January 2022).

Whitmore, J (2002) *Coaching for Performance: Growing People, Performance and Purpose*. Boston, MA: Nicholas Brearley.

Dr Arcadia Woods

Arcadia Woods joined the University of Bradford in November 2019 and, as part of the Student Experience and Success Team, has developed the Student Success Coach role at the institution. She has over eight years' experience of working in higher education as a researcher, teacher and personal tutor. Arcadia's interests include student success and retention in higher education, student engagement, widening participation, student well-being, and assessment and feedback for learning. Arcadia is a Fellow of the Higher Education Academy.

Ruth Lefever

Ruth Lefever joined the University of Bradford in 2009 as a researcher and has over 15 years' experience working in higher education. Her previous research and activity covered the first-year experience, student retention, welfare and support, student representation, widening participation, internationalisation and student resilience. Ruth's current work focuses on student engagement, supporting transitions into and through university, staff/student partnerships and peer support. Her particular interests include student peer community building, qualitative research, notions of belonging and gender. Ruth is a Bradford Teaching Fellow, a Senior Fellow of the Higher Education Academy and sits on the International Academic Peer Learning Leadership Group.

Case study 24
Introducing group personal tutoring to improve student engagement

Janet Wright

Themes	Page number locations in the companion book
Developing a sense of belonging among students	13
Embedded into teaching	22
Group personal tutoring and advising	114–17
Personal tutoring and advising curriculum	122–8
Student engagement	44, 56, 57, 58–60, 66–7
Student involvement and co-creation	61, 107, 116, 167–8
Student peer support	61, 107, 116

Introduction

In 2019 we introduced a new personal tutoring programme for undergraduates which replaced one-to-one meetings with group personal tutoring. This new programme was part of a wider project, led by our Widening Participation Success Working Group, to consider how to design content in programmes to develop students' resilience and resourcefulness.

The University of Law student body

The University of Law is one of the UK's longest-established specialist providers of legal education. We launched our first undergraduate degree, the Bachelor of Laws (LLB), in 2012 and currently have over 14,000 students enrolled across nine UK campuses, with satellite campuses at seven other universities, two overseas campuses and an online campus. Our undergraduate population comprises just over 3000 students studying law, business, criminology and policing. A high proportion of undergraduate students are from a widening participation background with 56 per cent of students from a Black, Asian or Minority Ethnic (BAME) background and just under 53 per cent of students from Index of Multiple Deprivation (IMD) groups 1 and 2 (the most deprived areas).

Why was there a need for personal tutoring to change?

Our undergraduate programmes initially adopted the same personal tutoring model as our postgraduate programmes: a series of individual appointments between the tutor and student. While this approach had been successful for postgraduates, attendance figures showed that many new undergraduates were not engaging with the individual meetings and student survey results evidenced a lack of a sense of belonging (The University of Law, 2019), something that is crucial to student success (Thomas, 2012). We recognised it was key for personal tutors to support students in their transition to university and help them engage at an early stage (Wilcox et al, 2005) and that students would benefit from a structured approach to personal tutoring (Thomas, 2006).

Set against the backdrop of a finding by The Insight Network (nd) and Dig-In (nd) that 87 per cent of students reported struggling with feelings of anxiety (Bottell, 2019), we had concerns about the mental health and well-being of our students and saw an increase in the proportion of students reporting mental health difficulties. We also noticed a trend for students to disengage as their studies became more demanding.

Students reported, via staff–student liaison committee meetings, that they felt intimidated by one-to-one meetings with tutors and would feel more comfortable with peers present. They were either not attending meetings or, if they did attend, they were not revealing the information which may have helped them obtain the support needed. Students also felt overwhelmed with the volume of information provided during induction and were not taking on board important messages about the availability of support services. We know that peer support can play an important role in resilience (McIntosh and Shaw, 2017) and therefore concluded that we should include group sessions in our personal tutoring and embed resilience into those sessions as part of an integrated curriculum model (Earwaker, 1992).

The new personal tutoring programme

The Students' Union was involved in the design of the new programme to capture the student voice. We also engaged an external consultant with expertise in developing resilience in young people. The consultant worked with us to design some activities in the sessions and also provided training for tutors.

Students continued to have an initial individual meeting with their personal tutor during induction to enable any confidential conversations to take place. Three group sessions of one hour were scheduled for Foundation Year and Year 1 students during their first six months of study and were timed to fit in with the lead up to formative assessments, the end of teaching and the start of semester 2. Students were in groups of around ten; this facilitated peer discussion but was a sufficiently small number so they felt comfortable sharing their thoughts.

The sessions were designed to provide practical guidance and encourage positive working habits and resilience (Stevenson, 2006). Key themes covered were settling in, workload management, assessment processes, reflection on performance and future plans. Activities were interactive with case studies and quizzes, for example a quiz on plagiarism and academic misconduct using Kahoot, and case studies on time management and preparing for assessments, which required the students to give advice on what individuals should do. Opportunities were also provided for students to reflect on an individual basis without sharing their thoughts unless they particularly wished to by, for example, writing down their achievements so far and giving advice to the person they were on their first day at university.

Students were still encouraged to meet with their personal tutor individually when they needed support and personal tutors continued to follow up with students if there were concerns. Individual meetings were also retained for subsequent years of study.

The success of the programme

After the third group session in January 2020, students were asked to complete a questionnaire to provide feedback. Eighty per cent of the students who attended the group sessions felt they had benefitted from learning confidence-building techniques in the sessions, 94 per cent reported they had subsequently set themselves action steps in order to achieve personal goals and 80 per cent had made use of the time management techniques covered in the sessions. Student awareness of the support services on offer also increased as a result of the sessions, particularly in relation to mental health, disability support and inclusion services. Verbatim comments from students were also very positive:

> *It gave me the courage and motivation to believe that my limiting factors won't stop me if I am determined to be successful and attain my ambitions.*

> *I feel more confident and better able to manage and deal with stress and workloads in order to achieve success.*

We conducted an analysis of student engagement in semester 1 assessments compared to the previous two academic intakes. There was a 17 per cent increase in students sitting assessments compared to previous cohorts and a 54 per cent increase in concession applications for absences due to mitigating circumstances (measured by analysing the percentage of concession applications made for absences in assessments). A concession application for absence in mitigating circumstances, if accepted, allows that student to sit the assessment as an additional first attempt and avoid their absence being treated as a fail and therefore their mark on a future attempt being capped.

Feedback was also sought from tutors who delivered the sessions. They found the sessions helped create a better bond with their personal tutees. This outcome was surprising as we had anticipated a reduction in the connection between the tutor and student with the loss of one-to-one meetings. Students were found to be more receptive to taking advice from each other, for example on seeking welfare or study skills support, than they were when directed to support services by staff. The attitude of the most engaged and positive students also seemed to influence other members of the group, leading to greater positivity among the cohort.

What problems did we encounter?

Student attendance at the sessions was relatively low with, on average, just 50 per cent of students attending. Reasons given by students for not attending were a lack of awareness of the sessions, despite these being timetabled, or the session not being at a convenient time for the individual. Although we had hoped the group sessions would be more efficient for tutors, time still needed to be spent meeting with students on a one-to-one basis to discuss more personal issues and chase up on non-attendance. We also found it challenging to schedule the sessions as there was less flexibility than with one-to-one appointments.

Lessons for other institutions

The response of both students and staff to the group personal tutoring sessions has, overall, been very positive and we have continued to run this programme. A clear increase in engagement with assessments led to more students being awarded additional first attempts for assessments when absent, which improves their chances of success and avoids students feeling a sense of failure.

Given the disruption and challenges young people have faced during the Covid-19 pandemic, the group sessions will in future provide a valuable means for students to share their experiences and learn how to deal with set-backs. The sessions have been successfully delivered to online cohorts and help foster a greater sense of community and belonging among students who would otherwise be working largely independently.

The challenge moving forward is to improve student engagement in the group sessions themselves. Further research needs to be undertaken in this area but the intention is to involve students who have benefitted from attending the group sessions to act as mentors to new students and encourage their engagement. We will also look carefully at the scheduling and publicity around the sessions.

From our experience, group personal tutoring should not fully replace one-to-one meetings between a student and their personal tutor; there is a need for confidential discussions to take place. As students progress through their studies, they need to gain more independence and discussions also need to be more tailored to the individual needs of the student. However, group sessions during a student's first year of undergraduate study provide a good mechanism for encouraging peer interactions outside of academic subjects. Carefully constructed activities in such sessions can have a positive effect on student confidence, resilience and engagement, for example by supporting students to recognise when they need help, encouraging them to seek help at an early stage and creating a positive mindset where they feel more confident in attempting assessments.

Key messages

Group personal tutoring can be an effective way to:

- improve student confidence;

- enable students to adopt a more positive approach to challenges;

- increase student awareness of support services;

- increase student engagement in assessments;

- improve the relationship between students and personal tutors.

Critical reflections

1. This case study identifies a number of benefits from students undertaking peer discussion and peer activities in group tutorials within their first year of undergraduate study. What other curricula and non-curricula activities might these benefits positively affect and how?

2. Would you plan any adaptations to facilitating a group tutorial session in comparison with any other group-based learning and teaching session? If yes, provide a rationale for each.

3. Develop an outline session plan for a group tutorial session which aims to improve your students' resilience in terms of knowledge, skills and attitude. Provide details on the following, as a minimum:

    - details of the students' level and discipline;

    - learning outcomes;

    - learning and teaching activities;

    - formative assessment and feedback strategies.

References

Bottell, J (2019) University Student Mental Health Survey 2018. [online] Available at: www.theinsightnetwork.co.uk/uncategorized/university-student-mental-health-survey-2018 (accessed 10 December 2021).

Dig-In (nd) [online] Available at: www.digin.co.uk (accessed 4 October 2021).

Earwaker, J (1992) *Helping and Supporting Students*. Buckingham: Society for Research into Higher Education and Open University Press.

McIntosh, E and Shaw, J (2017) Student Resilience: Exploring the Positive Case for Resilience. [online] Available at: www.unite-group.co.uk/universities/student-resilience-exploring-positive-case-resilience (accessed 10 December 2021).

Stevenson, N (2006) Integrating Personal Tutoring with Personal Development Planning. [online] Available at: www.advance-he.ac.uk/knowledge-hub/integrating-personal-tutoring-personal-development-planning (accessed 4 October 2021).

The Insight Network (nd) [online] Available at: www.theinsightnetwork.co.uk (accessed 4 October 2021).

The University of Law (2019) End of Year Survey 2019.

Thomas, L (2006) Widening Participation and the Increased Need for Personal Tutoring. In Thomas, L and Hixenbaugh, P (eds) *Personal Tutoring in Higher Education* (pp 21–31). Stoke-on-Trent: Trentham Books.

Thomas, L (2012) *Building Student Engagement and Belonging in Higher Education at a Time of Change. Final Report from the What Works? Student Retention and Success Programme.* [online] Available at: www.heacademy.ac.uk/sites/default/files/resources/What_works_final_report.pdf (accessed 10 December 2021).

Wilcox, P, Winn, S and Fyvie-Gauld, M (2005) It Was Nothing to Do with the University, It Was Just the People: The Role of Social Support in the First-year Experience of Higher Education. *Studies in Higher Education*, 30(6): 707–22.

Janet Wright

After reading law at Cambridge and an initial career as a solicitor, Janet Wright moved to the then College of Law (now The University of Law) to focus on training. She has held a variety of teaching and management roles at the university and is currently the Head of Undergraduate Programmes & Student Affairs with responsibility for the delivery and development of undergraduate programmes across the university. Janet is particularly interested in the provision of support to undergraduate students as well as improving student outcomes and is inspired by what her students can achieve, often in very challenging circumstances.

Case study 25

The 'Hero', the 'Professional' and the 'Nurturer': the challenge for personal tutoring to negotiate identities within systems of practice in higher education

Annabel Yale and Dawn Warren

Themes	Page number locations in the companion book
Boundaries between roles	53–73
Differentiating by subject area	–
Personal tutor and advisor forums	–
Reflective practice	153–67, 170–1
Role definition	12–14
Role types – expert versus generalist; senior and specialised personal tutor and advisor	22–3
Values in personal tutoring and advising	32–9

Introduction

Defining the role of the personal tutor (PT) is challenging given the constantly shifting higher education landscape. Universities attempt this through practice and policy documents; however, the lack of clarity on the role is complicated by the gap in professional development provision for personal tutors in UK higher education (for example, Walker, 2020). PTs express concerns over high workload, boundaries in relationships and the emotional consequences of supporting complex student needs without the necessary skills or experience (McFarlane, 2016). Given this complex context we wanted to explore how PTs negotiate the role and whether PTs differed in their practice. Our research aim was to use any new insights to inform PT practice via the Faculty Personal Tutor Forums which, in turn, would improve the student experience.

Our approach

We conducted the research in a post-1992 university in the north-west of England which typically has over 70 per cent of the student population from at least one underrepresented group. We conducted ten in-depth semi-structured interviews (March to June 2019) with PTs from early years, primary, secondary and further education departments across the Faculty of Education. All PTs who volunteered to participate had worked as PTs at the university for between six and 13 years.

We used interpretative phenomenological analysis (IPA) to analyse the interview data as it has the potential to provide meaningful insights into lived experiences, which can then be drawn on to inform practice and thinking (Smith et al, 2009). Consistent with IPA, we had an openness to what the data might mean. We drew on psychological theories, such as cognitive dissonance (Festinger, 1957) and those related to authenticity and well-being (Wood et al, 2008) to help us with our interpretations in trying to make sense of what personal tutors were telling us.

Interview questions included the following.

•   What makes a good personal tutor?

•   What are the positives, negatives and challenges of the role?

•   What is the purpose of personal tutoring?

•   In an ideal world, what would you change?

Findings

Through IPA we identified emergent themes which concerned the beliefs, values and tensions around the PT role. We were able to identify personal tutor identity as the superordinate theme that connected and encompassed the emergent themes. Within *personal tutor identity* we found three distinct professional identities (the 'Hero', the 'Professional' and the 'Nurturer') and team identity. Referring to our participants as p1–p10, we have included quotes based on their representativeness.

Personal tutor identity

PTs constructed their own professional identities which they draw on to guide their practice and to help negotiate the demands of the role on their time, energy and emotions. Identities were constructed from PTs' backgrounds and their values, beliefs and attitudes from their own cognate discipline. The challenge for many PTs is the conflict they feel when trying to address a system of personal tutoring which does not fit with their own professional identity and values.

Professional identity

Care and building relationships with students was important for all PTs but what care means to them and the nature of these relationships differed according to their different disciplines. *'You can't have a relationship with somebody you don't care about, can you?'* (p3).

The 'Heroes' were PTs on postgraduate courses and descriptions of themselves can be likened to the Greek god Atlas, holding up the course with their own hands with everyone under their all-seeing eye and protection. They feel this is a product of the demands of the course, high student numbers and that all other tutors are part-time so therefore are not as available or flexible as students need them to be. They respond to emails from students outside of office hours and feel overburdened by student numbers but do not feel they have any choice.

> *I find it very hard to try to draw that line between teaching, personal tutoring or lecturing. Some would say, available more than I should be... the only constraining feature on my availability has been the numbers on the course.* (p10)

The 'Professionals' tended to be PTs on primary and secondary courses taking more of a direct coaching approach in their practice. Through timetabled and structured meetings, PTs ask prompt questions to identify targets (with students taking ownership of these in a feedback loop) and talk in terms of developing the academic and personal resilience of their students.

> *It's not caring as in, I don't want to be a substitute mother figure... it's caring as a way of supporting, and guiding through an educational journey, an educational process, and it's what all relationships are built on for me.* (p3)

The 'Nurturers' tended to be PTs in early years who draw on its language and practices to care for and nurture their students. They talk of providing warmth and safety through positive relationships, having a playful yet professional approach, treating students as unique individuals, enabling their students to grow and helping students to remove any barriers to their learning. One PT describes the approach she takes to struggling students: *'I'm kind of scooping them up, dusting them off... it's kind of like a warm hug without the hug'* (p6).

Team identity

We found that a shared team identity and vision was underpinned by the kind of professionals that PTs wanted students to be, defined by their discipline. Personal tutoring is regarded as a mechanism to guide and support students towards this professional identity. They recognised the positive impact of a cohesive team approach on student outcomes and shared their frustrations when leadership decisions were made that affected this.

Everything is very disparate and there isn't a really strong sense of team... it can be quite hard to get people together because they're working on every programme but, where you get that buy-in from the tutors, the success of it can be phenomenal. I mean, if you look at the outcomes of the students on those programmes, that's down to the team of personal tutors. (p8)

Personal tutors frequently described the conflict between an enforced system of personal tutoring and what they felt mattered to them: building relationships and caring about students. Being at odds with the system meant that some personal tutors struggled to retain an authentic self. *'I don't disagree with anything on paper but the system seems to actively work against it'* (p8). This is a concern, as there is a strong correlation in research between authenticity and well-being (Wood et al, 2008), suggesting that acting in ways that are not authentic may damage well-being. Acting inauthentically, where there is incongruence between our deeper values and actions, leads to an emotional force that seeks reduction (Lenton et al, 2013). Where this is the case for PTs, they seem to agonise over these conflicts.

Impact

We shared our insights with personal tutors across departments at a faculty level through the Personal Tutor Forums. Forums occur every three months and although not mandatory, around a third of the Faculty typically attend (50–60 colleagues).

We suggested PTs start by creating a safe space for reflection and open dialogue to prompt meaningful discussions around what matters to them (their core values and beliefs). Teams should aim to create a shared understanding of professionalism as PTs, consider how they can build a more cohesive and coherent team identity, and take ownership of this at the programme level. This would also allow for PTs to negotiate their own identities within a shared identity and reduce any internal conflict. PTs were encouraged to reflect on their own identities and how their discipline and experience informs their practice. By making these explicit, tutors will have a better understanding of their role as a PT within their specific department.

Feedback from the evaluations so far has been mostly positive. PTs said they have a better understanding of their own practice and that this has evolved through sharing and listening to others exploring theirs. PTs really valued the opportunity to talk and share openly about what they do and although there may be differences between PTs, the discussion helped to develop a shared coherence in their values around the role. PTs felt more confident in their own practice after listening to others negotiate some of the tensions in the role. The biggest barrier for some seemed to be in the initial creating of a safe space where PTs felt they could talk openly. We are currently seeking feedback on this to provide more support and suggestions for those struggling via the next forum.

Conclusion

Creating opportunities for personal tutors to talk about their different PT experiences allows tutors to find their voice, negotiate their thinking and resolve any internal conflicts between the systems and processes that dictate PT practice, and their own values and beliefs. This should provide the reassurance that is often needed when responding to increasingly challenging and complex student issues. Adopting this approach will enable PTs to gain a truer sense of themselves, to better understand why they do what they do, offering a sense of coherence for these shifting roles to co-exist without conflict. Feeling authentic in their actions, PTs will be in a stronger position to articulate their role effectively with their students, providing clear rationales for expectations and boundaries of the role. Our aim is to conduct focus sessions with students in the next academic year across programmes to assess the impact of our initiative on the student experience of personal tutoring.

Key messages

- Undertake development work to gain insights into what informs approaches to practice.

- Help personal tutors to reflect on their own identities and to consider how these are influenced by their own experiences, background and discipline.

- Recognise that PT practice can differ on the basis of discipline – a *one-size-fits-all* approach is not effective.

- Encourage teams to develop their own PT culture specific to their programme.

Critical reflections

1. How would you explain your own personal tutor identity? Consider including your personal and/or professional values, beliefs, attitudes and how your experience and discipline might influence your identity.

2. Do you recognise the three professional identities in the case study within your own practice or other personal tutors? Does your own identity from Question 1 closely align with one or more of these and how? If not, how would you encapsulate your own personal tutor identity in a name?

3. Do you feel that your own discipline affects your personal tutoring practice and how? How would you describe 'the kind of professionals' that you want your students to be? How do you feel this compares with other personal tutors within your discipline?

References

Festinger, L (1957) *Cognitive Dissonance Theory*. Newbury Park: SAGE.

Lenton, A P, Bruder, M, Slabu, L and Sedikides, C (2013) How Does "Being Real" Feel? The Experience of State Authenticity. *Journal of Personality*, 81: 276–89.

McFarlane, K J (2016) Tutoring the Tutors: Supporting Effective Personal Tutoring. *Active Learning in Higher Education*, 17(1): 77–88.

Smith, J A, Flowers, P and Larkin, M (2009) *Interpretative Phenomenological Analysis: Theory, Method and Research*. London: SAGE.

Walker, B W (2020) Tackling the Personal Tutoring Conundrum: A Qualitative Study on the Impact of Developmental Support for Tutors. *Active Learning in Higher Education*. [online] Available at: https://doi.org/10.1177/1469787420926007 (accessed 14 January 2022).

Wood, A M, Linley, P A, Maltby, J, Baliousis, M and Joseph, S (2008) The Authentic Personality: A Theoretical and Empirical Conceptualization and the Development of the Authenticity Scale. *Journal of Counselling Psychology*, 55: 385–99.

Dr Annabel Yale

Annabel Yale is a Lecturer in Early Years and completed her PhD in July 2018 on *The Student Experience of Personal Tutoring*. Her background is psychology and social sciences and she has expertise in both quantitative and qualitative research methods. Annabel has published research on the student experience and expectations of personal tutoring, and in her most recent article explored the usefulness of the psychological contract in understanding student expectations. She is actively researching the experiences of personal tutoring from the perspective of both students and personal tutors. Annabel is also a Fellow of the Higher Education Academy.

Dawn Warren

Dawn Warren is an Assistant Head in a large department in the Faculty of Education at Edge Hill University. She is responsible for student experience and engagement, recruitment, retention and employability. Dawn's work is shaped by the stages of the student journey, from 'first contact' through to 'life after study', and aims to identify, evaluate and disseminate good practice in the improvement and enhancement of the student experience. She is actively researching the experiences of personal tutoring from the perspective of both students and personal tutors. Dawn is also a Fellow of the Higher Education Academy.

About UKAT   UKAT

The UK Advising and Tutoring association (UKAT) is delighted to be associated with the production of this volume of collected practice and experience. It shows the rich variety of ways in which personal tutoring can be provided, and clearly shows the impact of personal tutoring in supporting student outcomes and success. It will be a useful reference for practitioners for many years to come.

UKAT is a charitable trust and membership association representing personal tutors and academic advisors in the UK higher education sector. Our mission is to advance effective personal tutoring and academic advising practice within higher education so that every higher education student can experience inclusiveness, well-being and personal growth, leading them to flourish and succeed.

UKAT membership is open to higher education institutions, individual tutors and advisors, and students. Our diverse membership consists of academics, administrators, students, researchers, professional advisors, counsellors and others who are committed to enhancing their students' educational development through high-quality advising and tutoring. Members are drawn from all regions of the UK and beyond and belong to institutions from across the spectrum of higher and further education; they bring to the association a wide range of experience and different perspectives.

We work closely with our member institutions and individual members to enhance advising practice through standards and frameworks, professional development events, online learning, conferences and webinars, consultancy services, publications, and resources. Recognising that effective personal tutoring and academic advising is at the core of student success, UKAT aspires to lead the development and dissemination of innovative theory, research, and practice of student advising and tutoring in the UK and beyond. We encourage practitioners to engage with the scholarship of personal tutoring and to adopt a scholarly-informed approach to their practice.

Our flagship Professional Recognition Scheme (www.ukat.ac.uk/recognition) aims to raise the profile of personal tutoring and the impact that it has in supporting student success, and in improving student engagement and improved outcomes for all students. This developmental scheme is open to anyone providing personal tutoring or academic advising to higher education students. It enables individuals to demonstrate competency in personal tutoring practice at three distinct levels – *Recognised Practitioner in Advising, Recognised Senior Advisor* and *Recognised Leader in Advising* – referenced against the UKAT Professional Framework for Academic Advising and Personal Tutoring (www.ukat.ac.uk/framework). Supporting their staff to gain recognition through the scheme enables higher education institutions to prove how they intentionally provide holistic support to learners and how they work to improve student success and outcomes for all students. Participation in the scheme offers a proactive way to develop staff, enabling institutions to address key goals and drivers articulated in institutional strategy, Access and Participation plans and higher education policy. To date, 29 higher education institutions have participated in the scheme. Some use it as an adjunct to Advance HE's HEA Fellowship scheme, and a way to ensure that HEA Fellows remain in good standing.

UKAT has 25 member institutions, which together constitute an Advisory Board that informs the strategy and activities of UKAT to ensure that it remains relevant to the needs of students and higher education providers. Students are the heart, and ultimate benefactors, of everything that UKAT does, which is why we encourage student representation among our membership, and partnership working with students through our Advisory Board and UKAT events. Many of our events, including our free monthly webinar series, are open to anyone. Members receive access to exclusive information and resources, and discounted rates for conference and event registration, professional development courses, and professional recognition applications.

For more information about UKAT and to get involved in our activities, please visit www.ukat.ac.uk.

Index